Praise for *Cross-Cultural Conflict*

"From his wealth of experience at home and abroad, Duane Elmer has
created a wondrous tribute to the human capability of learning
to relate to people who are different. Dr. Elmer's easy-going style of
storytelling makes *Cross-Cultural Conflict: Building Relationships
for Effective Ministry* easy to read and understand.
He makes excellent use of biblical material, both as principles
and as practical applications. The truth that motivates
the book is deep and sound: God created human diversity;
thus we can learn to celebrate it rather than to avoid or fear it."

Ted Ward
Trinity Evangelical Divinity School

"Dr. Elmer has addressed the basic problem behind ninety percent of
all my frustrations as a mission executive. His insights reflect both
a compassion for world missions and a solid understanding of social
science research. I will encourage our SIM directors to read
and discuss the book. I highly recommend the book as required
reading for new missionaries. Thank you for this most
important contribution to world missions."

James E. Plueddemann
SIM International

"After twenty-five years of missionary work, I realize the importance of
cultural sensitivity for Christian workers. Every cross-cultural
worker and those who live in multicultural communities
will find this book informative and helpful in
adjusting to another culture. All missionary candidates
should read this book before they go out to mission fields."

Bong Rin Ro
Overseas Missionary Fellowship

"Considering the fact that much of mission work has to do with
relationships, and whenever significant relationship is
attempted there is bound to appear conflict, this book will prove
to be an invaluable tool for cross-cultural workers."

David Tai-Woong Lee
Global Ministry Training Center

"Duane Elmer offers not only a comprehensible picture of the nature of culture and conflict but also practical handles for preventive and corrective ways to handle conflicts and build healthy relationships. This book should be required reading for any person involved in or entering into cross-cultural ministry. However, it has enormous value for anyone interested in building healthy relationships to serve God more effectively, wherever they may be."

Luis Bush
AD2000 and Beyond

"This book effectively bridges the gap which separates our theology from our cultural reality. It reveals some of the causes of conflicts . . . and offers ways of solving them, as well as ways to avoid potential conflicts that arise from the misunderstanding of other cultures. The book brings to the surface hidden cultural values which create tension or conflict in the workplace, in cross-cultural ministries and in societies in general."

Alemu Beeftu
Compassion International

"The strength of Elmer's book is in its use of actual life stories and a wealth of stories and proverbs from many cultures, as well as the sections on managing conflict in cultures where avoiding shame, saving face and preserving honor are of highest value.

"This work should be in every ministry library. Any cross-cultural ministry would profit greatly from this book, particularly in reference to cross-cultural staffing and in the outside relationships so vital to ministry."

John H. Orme
IFMA

"Dr. Elmer presents biblically based, thoroughly researched and practical solutions to this world's most recognized malady. . . . This book is a *must* for every Christ-centered believer who wants to thrive in this decade and into the start of the next millennium."

Wayne Shabaz
consultant to multi-national corporations
on global diversity

CROSS-CULTURAL CONFLICT

Building Relationships for Effective Ministry

DUANE ELMER

INTERVARSITY PRESS
DOWNERS GROVE, ILLINOIS 60515

©1993 by Duane H. Elmer

InterVarsity Press® is the book-publishing division of InterVarsity Christian Fellowship®, a student movement active on campus at hundreds of universities, colleges and schools of nursing in the United States of America, and a member movement of the International Fellowship of Evangelical Students. For information about local and regional activities, write Public Relations Dept., InterVarsity Christian Fellowship, 6400 Schroeder Rd., P.O. Box 7895, Madison, WI 53707-7895.

ISBN 0-8308-1657-7

Printed in the United States of America ♾

Library of Congress Cataloging-in-Publication Data.

Elmer, Duane, 1943-
  Cross-cultural conflict: building relationships for effective
ministry/Duane Elmer.
    p.   cm.
    Includes bibliographical references.
    ISBN 0-8308-1657-7 (alk. paper)
    1. Missionaries—Training of. 2. Conflict management—Religious
aspects—Christianity. 3. Intergroup relations. I. Title.
  BV2091.E55   1993
261.8'34—dc20   *93-41901*
                                                                          CIP

15   14   13   12   11   10   9   8   7   6   5   4

04   03   02   01   00   99   98   97

*This book
is dedicated*

*to
Muriel
a superb example
of grace
in relationships*

PART 1

UNDERSTANDING CONFLICT AND CULTURE

1

THE AMAZING CONTOURS OF CONFLICT

It may be difficult to teach a person to respect another unless we can help people to see things from the other's point of view.
KOHEI GOSHI

It was Sunday morning in the sleepy town of Amanzimtoti on South Africa's picturesque Indian Ocean coast. The heat was very intense. A light ocean breeze offered some relief, but I hardly noticed. I was scheduled to preach at a local church and was afraid of arriving late. My directions to the church were not too clear. I never quite knew what to expect when I visited a church for the first time. Sometimes church services would be held in a garage, sometimes under a big flamboyant tree spreading a huge umbrella of shade, sometimes in a town hall, sometimes in a tent attached to a residence. The people of rural South Africa possessed boundless ingenuity for creating worship spaces.

It being Sunday, the stores were all closed. And since the extreme heat was keeping pedestrian traffic to a minimum, my most likely source for information on the church's whereabouts would be an attendant at a petrol (gas) station.

The service was to begin in a few minutes, and I was getting desperate. I spotted a petrol station and pulled in. Inevitably, the attendant was black (black workers have historically filled the unskilled jobs in this land of apartheid). The attendant came out and offered a courteous greeting. I quickly explained my problem and requested his help. Did he know the place I was searching for?

He stood up straight and looked left, then right, his right hand touching his chin reflectively. It seemed clear to me. He was looking back and forth to assess how best to direct me to my destination.

He gave me directions, and I raced off in accord with his verbal map, breathing easier. In a few minutes, though, it became clear that his help was taking me even farther from my destination. I stewed in frustration: Why had he steered me wrong? Now I would suffer certain embarrassment for tardiness. If he didn't know the location of the church, why hadn't he just said so? If he did know, why had he sent me on this wild goose chase in the opposite direction? It was so unfair.

Clearly, the man was either irresponsible, dishonest or downright devious. I had been trained to "think the best about the other person" and to follow biblical injunctions to "honor one another above yourselves." But surely these rules didn't have to be followed when one was dealing with people who, it seemed, were deliberately deceptive.

Gaining Perspective

When I first moved to South Africa, I had little understanding of cultural values other than my own. As a result, accurate interpretation of other people's actions was nearly impossible. I could see only through my own cultural lenses. I needed to learn and adapt to the cultural lenses of the local people. That would require not setting my lenses aside, but adding theirs to mine. I did not need to give up my own cultural frame of reference to accept and appreciate one different from mine.

Like everyone else, I tend to be egocentric (that is, I believe my perspective is correct and better than yours; so I make little or no effort to understand yours). I simply assume that since I have an extensive education and other symbols of superiority, my judgments are better. I don't really think much about this assumption; it is just there.

But if I am willing to pay the price to learn another's cultural frame of reference, I can avoid many conflicts—and in the end, I will find myself the richer for it. In fact, we all need to gain understanding of other cultures, even if we never plan to leave the country we were born in. As our cities become more and more culturally diverse, multiculturalism is fast becoming a survival skill.

Biblical Insights

There are sound theological reasons for committing ourselves to understand other cultures and appreciate them wherever possible. Making that commitment will unfold for us new and wonderful dimensions of God's character, for our God can be properly revealed only through diversity.

When God had finished creating the world, he looked at the "vast array" (Gen 2:1) and announced that "it was very good" (Gen 1:31). To celebrate creation is to celebrate diversity, including diversities of people. And we cannot celebrate out of ignorance. Genuine celebration comes from genuine appreciation. This requires learning and understanding, and these are incompatible with egocentrism and superiority.

All people bear the image of God (Gen 1:27). To learn of them and from them with an open mind is to discover how God reveals something of himself through their distinct world and life view. As we know, all people have been injured by the Fall, by sin's hold on the world. Yet God's grace is present in all people and in all cultures. As we submit ourselves to learning from other cultures, we catch glimpses of God's grace that would be unavailable in our own culture.

We are called to love all people. But can I truly love someone I do not, at least in some measure, understand? Love requires some understanding of its object. That means love is *culturally defined.* When we truly love others, we love them in their own context, in keeping with the way they define love. We can't express love in a vacuum. It can be expressed *egocentrically* (my way) or *sociocentrically* (as the other person would define an act of love).

I am a North American, and in North America we have defined ways of showing friendship and love. One of those ways is to invite someone to my house for an evening meal together; we set a day and time for this meeting. Both parties understand this as a friendly, if not loving, act and something that will strengthen our relationship.

But in many parts of Africa, an invitation to come to my house at a designated time may not be interpreted as friendly and loving. In fact, it might be interpreted as a sign that I want a formal, distant relationship. Why?

In Africa one shows friendship by stopping in unannounced, perhaps at mealtime. If a time, place and agenda for meeting have to be prearranged, the relationship cannot be open and spontaneous and evolve naturally, or so the reasoning goes. Love is culturally defined.

Refreshing Cultural Insights
Gaining a new set of cultural lenses will bring a more accurate interpretation of cross-cultural conflict situations, like my problem with the wrong directions to church. The better we are at interpreting culture, the fewer conflicts we will experience, the more we will be able to build authentic relationships, and the greater will be our ability to communicate God's truth.

Let me ask you a question. Which is the greater sin: to tell a lie or to lose your temper? Take a moment to think about your answer, then register it in your mind. Take the question at face value; don't argue that all sin is equally abhorrent before God. Now, what is your answer?

Consider why you chose that particular answer. Why does your choice represent the greater sin? Suppose someone else chose the other answer. What possible reason(s) could support that choice?

Don't rush through this; it's very important. Take time to think it out.

In doing so you begin a process of cultural understanding that will be repeated thousands of times as you adjust to and minister in another culture.

Let me make a guess at your answer. If you are a North American or from Western Europe, and especially if you have white skin, you chose lying as the greater sin. If you are from another part of the world, my guess is that you chose losing your temper as the greater sin. If you are from the Western world (North America or Europe) but a person of color, you may have had difficulty choosing, since your heritage may allow you to offer reasoned argument for either answer.

Of course, here the real issue is not which answer is correct but why you perceive a given answer to be correct. In Western culture, especially among Western white people, a very high value is placed on accuracy and truth. So lying is the greater sin. Outside the Western world, for the most part, greater value is placed on relationships. Losing one's temper is a more grievous sin, because it represents a rupture in relationship.

You may argue that truth should be a higher value than relationship, but the reality is that the majority of the world thinks differently. That does not make the majority right, but it does suggest that it might be wise to try to understand why they see it that way.

How much does God value relationships? How much does he value truth?

Back to the Petrol Station

What does this have to do with a black petrol-station attendant's giving me inaccurate directions? Here is the connection. In this context relationship is valued over truth. African culture typically places great value on courtesy to the stranger and help to the needy. I qualified as both a stranger and a needy person. The last thing the attendant wanted to do was disappoint someone who was looking to him for assistance, and especially when he sensed it was assistance I urgently needed. So rather than disappoint me by not being able to help, and rather than risk my thinking poorly of him, he gave me his best effort.

But there is more. In much of Africa, as well as in other parts of the world, not losing face is an important cultural value. It corresponds loosely to the Western idea of avoiding personal humiliation or embarrassment, but is far more compelling and powerful in determining behavior. We will examine this issue more closely later. The attendant wanted to avoid disappointing me in order to uphold the cultural value of courtesy and helping those in need. To admit that he did not have what I needed was to bring shame or loss of face upon himself. Both situations represented cultural taboos and would be avoided at whatever cost.

One last factor should be noted. The overwhelming majority of black people in South Africa traveled (and still do) either by foot or by public transportation. Riding a meandering bus or a speeding train, one rarely pays attention to street names. Paths often do not follow roads; even if they do, the names of the streets are rarely useful. Besides, following street names requires being able to read. Distances are measured in walking time, not driving time. Walkers use a very different set of words when giving directions (assuming they know precisely the destination) from those of a person in an automobile. The walker uses trees, rocks, hills, ditches and buildings as guideposts. The driver, however, relies on miles, number of traffic lights, street signs, blocks, building numbers and cross streets.

In retrospect, it may seem foolish that I imputed dishonesty or malice to the petrol-station attendant. But it only seems foolish now . . . now that I understand his cultural frame of reference. I learned it is unwise to make quick judgments about people's motives and character. It takes time, conversations, questions, listening and the whole range of learning skills to form accurate perceptions about people who are different from me. I must suspend judgment, maintain an open mind and seek more information (especially from those people I am prone to judge) before drawing conclusions. If I am too quick to judge or draw a conclusion, my mind closes, learning stops, and the potential for building a relationship is lost. My assessment of others must be a conscious, intentional process, or I am likely to slip into my old habits and to do an injustice to people whom Christ loves and for whom he died.

You may never go to South Africa or even to the continent of Africa and may be wondering why you need to be concerned about cross-cultural communication. The answer is simple: wherever you go (even down the street from your home), you experience cultural differences that have the potential to become cultural conflict. You need to know how to handle these differences; otherwise you may well become mired in misunderstanding and conflict. If you try to manage conflict from your own frame of reference, there is a good chance you will make things worse, even if your intentions are good. Thus begins a cycle of confusion that leads to further frustration and stress, if not alienation, in the relationship.

Avoid the cycle altogether. Learn to put on that other set of lenses. It takes patience, but it's not hard to do.

The Reasoning of a Novice

During my early years in Africa I often traveled to new places on Sundays, and the story about the petrol-station attendant recurred with agonizing consistency. I began to conclude that black people were at best highly unreliable, and at worst malicious toward white people (especially this one). It was hard not to believe the worst of them. I could think of no positive explanation for such behavior.

So I constructed a reasoning that at least made some sense to me but was less than complimentary to petrol attendants. This is how it went: In the apartheid system, black people are clearly the oppressed group; they have few creature comforts and often live in severe poverty. For this group of people, the burden of living in oppression and poverty must become unbearable. It is easy to see that an occasional misdirection to a white motorist would ever so slightly tip the scale of injustice and provide momentary release from the grip of powerlessness. At least, this was the reasoning I employed in my immature attempts to understand the problem.

These early experiences with cross-cultural conflict had an eroding effect on my view of an entire group of black South Africans. If you cannot trust people to be honest in giving directions, can you trust them in any sphere? Since I was unable to understand the cultural dynamics of this group of people, conflict led me into suspicion and distrust. It was not an intentional or even conscious process, but seemed to unfold quite naturally from the accumulating evidence. Over time, my observations took on the appearance of being factual.

Eventually, I realized my behavior was a result of the virus that resides in all of us. It is called prejudice, and when it infects large parts of the person, it properly falls in the category of racism. The biblical name for it is *sin*.

Ambiguity, Confusion and the Workings of the Mind

The mind naturally seeks to understand conflict situations, even minor ones. When facts are not immediately forthcoming to explain ambiguous situations, the mind tends to fill in the blanks. That is, we supply our own data to explain the situation. The fatal flaw is that we provide the understanding from *our* cultural frame of reference, not from the cultural frame of reference of the other person, or the situation in which the conflict exists.

The Western mind finds particular delight in providing answers to questions. An unanswered question is scandalous, so the mind quickly supplies its own answer from its own form of logic, its own cultural assumptions and its own value system. Westerners with a limited ability to tolerate ambiguity, suspend judgment and seek understanding from within other cultures create conflict situations where there are none and turn small conflicts into large ones.

I was feeling quite justified in judging black people in South Africa as uninformed, irresponsible, deceptive or malicious toward whites. Eventually I encountered similar situations in Zimbabwe (then Rhodesia) and Swaziland. The evidence now suggested the problem was more pervasive than just black people in South Africa.

Generalizations came so easily. So did stereotypes. Increasingly I was inclined to mistrust black people in South Africa, maybe anywhere. Suspicion feeds suspicion, and I began to notice only the "facts" that confirmed my emerging convictions. Before long I was failing to distinguish between the facts and my interpretation of the facts. They conveniently became one and the same. Yet what I saw as fact was radically affected by the cultural lenses I wore.

Most of this process is just below conscious level, but discernible to the alert and informed person. Unfortunately, at a certain point the process becomes self-perpetuating, on automatic pilot as it were. A measure of security comes when I know which "box" a person fits into, because then I know how to treat him or her. I do not need to get acquainted with the person before I judge him or her. At that point I have begun to treat people like objects and no longer see each one as a unique, esteemed human being designed by God and worthy of my individualized and respectful attention.

How We Fill In the Blanks

Social scientists have discovered an interesting behavior that tends to arise in situations of ambiguity or conflict. As I have already mentioned, when someone does something that we do not understand, and an explanation is not quickly forthcoming, we actually provide our own explanation. We fill in the blanks, so to speak. So when I was confused by the directions from the petrol attendant and no explanation was available to alleviate my confusion, I made up my own interpretation of the facts.

But here is the curious part. The interpretation we provide virtually always attributes a *negative* characteristic and motivation to the other person. We rarely give people the benefit of the doubt when they do something we don't understand. Since the Western mind needs immediate closure to ambiguities, Westerners are especially quick to attach some deficiency to the other person whenever confusion arises. You can easily see how this creates conflict when there was none, or aggravates minor conflicts into major ones.

Learning from Mistakes

In the case of the various black people who gave me errant directions, I made several mistakes. First, I confused the facts with my interpretation of the facts. It was fact that they often gave inaccurate information. What was not fact was that it happened because of some negative feature of their character or motivation. This was a premature conclusion on my part. It fulfilled my need for immediate answers, but did an injustice to the people because it was a prejudgment.

Second, because my culture had taught me to make quick decisions and judgments, I was not able to keep my mind open to culturally appropriate explanations. Nor was I inclined to seek them. Once I made a judgment in the matter, my mind closed. And then it reopened only to receive data that confirmed my inaccurate conclusion.

Third, my interpretation of the facts was heavily biased by my own cultural values. I was prone to supply answers that made the most sense in my cultural context. While this provided me with a certain measure of satisfaction, it only delayed the point at which I would need to deal with reality. An awareness of reality came when I began to learn about the Africans' culture and see, little by little, through their cultural lenses. More and more the answers I needed were supplied from their frame of reference and accurately reflected the true character and motivation of the people.

Fourth, once I felt justified in my conclusion, I unconsciously looked for further data to support it. At the same time, I failed to take note of data that could have contradicted or modified my conclusion. So I was stuck with a false conclusion for years. Conclusions and judgments seem to have a built-in permanence, even perpetuation, so we need to exercise extreme caution when making them.

These four mistakes can yield devastating results over the long term. By far the worst result is a diminished view of people and an inflated view of one's self—indicating an attitude of superiority. This emergence of superiority marks the end of trust, not in an absolute sense, but in terms of authentic fellowship with other members of the body of Christ.

If this kind of mindset can develop through a series of circumstances and misinterpretations surrounding something as simple as getting directions from petrol attendants, then it can be repeated in multitudes of other situations with unnerving ease.

This Book's Purpose and Scope

In our global village, cultures and racial groups are increasingly bumping into each other, causing misunderstanding and conflict. Cultural differences, coupled with everyone's natural tendency to "do it my way," make conflict inevitable. This means the ability to understand and respond wisely to conflict becomes a compelling priority for survival, peace and happiness in the emerging world of business, travel and mission.

Worldwide, cross-cultural interactions multiply daily through increased business transactions, deployment of military personnel, missionary activity, study abroad and tourism. The United States and many other countries are on the threshold of becoming nations of minorities. Boards, salespeople, executives, church staffs and mission agencies are forced to deal with cultural diversity and the inevitable misunderstandings that come from our different frames of reference.

One thing is certain: it is not business as usual. The rules each individual, as well as each culture, uses to manage conflict are not the same as other individuals and groups were taught to use. Each assumes its own rules are superior. Therein lies the first problem. Each is largely unaware of the rules by which it tries to manage conflict. Therein lies the second problem. Each culture has an intricate network of values that support the rules people use to handle conflict, so that understanding of these differences is far more complex than one first supposes. Therein lies the third problem.

Most cross-cultural conflicts are not intentional. Most are inadvertent, occurring because underlying cultural values and corresponding rules are not understood. What is surprising is not that we have so many conflicts but that, given everyone's cultural centeredness, there are not more conflicts.

This book is intended to clarify issues in intercultural and interracial conflict, to provide insights on the different ways people of various cultures handle conflict, to evaluate these according to Scripture and to provide practical guidelines for (1) helping us live more harmoniously with our cultural differences, (2) developing a positive strategy for dealing with conflict and (3) communicating the gospel of Jesus Christ more effectively and ministering the nurturing grace of God.

2
CULTURAL DIVERSITY WAS GOD'S IDEA
(AND SO WAS UNITY)

One sparrow does not make spring.
LATIN AMERICAN PROVERB

It was God who authored human diversity. This fact calls all of us to deal with cultural diversity, see it as he sees it—as good—and honor it as the handiwork of the wise and sovereign Creator.

Most of us do not welcome diversity into our lives. It forces us to change, disrupts our cozy patterns, engages us in a world where our deficiencies are exposed. Yet for all the less than appealing features of cultural and ethnic variety, important insights about God and his world go undiscovered if we avoid creative engagement with human diversity.

It Was Very Good

After completing the creation, God looked around, saw a vast array of diversity in all he had created and declared it "very good" (Gen 1:31). Diversity is rooted in the creative activity of God. But one wonders, Why?

For what reason did God display such variety in his human, plant, animal and inorganic world? It is my conviction that only in this immense and grand variety could we begin to capture the character, grace and glory of God. Put another way, God cannot adequately be revealed in a creation of similarities.

Thus in the process of learning about other cultures, affirming our various ethnic heritages and honoring (if not celebrating) diversity, we enlarge our appreciation for God, who in authoring diversity was trying to tell us about himself. Perhaps we are most like God when we also look around and affirm as good peoples and traditions different from our own and diligently seek to appreciate the beauty God has chosen to express in others.

The very differences God pronounced "very good" are also the greatest threat to Christian unity. Differences can build stronger bonds between people or it can break them. Broken relationships often result from a failure to understand and adjust to the differences we have inherited from a wise God.

Certainly not everything that belongs to your tradition or mine is good. Much has been contaminated by sin and needs to be either eliminated from our lives or reclaimed for the glory of God. Sin makes the effort of building unity across diversity more difficult but not impossible.

My experiences suggest that the large majority of conflicts resulting in brokenness are caused neither by core theological values being threatened nor by overt sin. Most conflicts that disrupt our lives grow out of innocent misunderstandings, unmet expectations, failure to get all the facts, or minor irritations that fester and become problems. If this is true, then we need to remind ourselves how important it is to deal effectively with conflict, since neglect brings pain and potential separation from those we love. We need to reconsider the biblical teaching on the unity of God's people and how it reflects his glory and affects the carrying out of his mission in this world.

Conflict, Unity and the Gospel

The Western world does not place a high premium on unity. Wherever individualism reigns supreme, community is easily sacrificed for personal preferences. Although I enjoy the luxuries of individualism, I cannot help but feel that it has also brought a certain impoverishment. Too quickly we splinter churches, friendships, families, and groups rather than struggle for ways to bridge differences, reconnect, forgive, reconcile and heal.

Individualism fosters an impatience with people and institutions: we can always join another church, find new friends or get another job. As long as we have options, we do not need to work at preserving our present relationships. At any sign of discomfort we jettison them and start over with someone else.

The dubious luxury of disposable relationships has a dark side—a serious dark side. We can afford to take the unity of believers lightly if other options are available and relatively painless. But failures in individual and community relationships cast aspersions on God's reputation. As a church splits, as a friendship dissolves, as a marriage ruptures, as colleagues become adversaries, the body of Christ fractures. These fractures are noticed by the unbelieving world. If God cannot keep his own people from becoming adversaries, why should a reflective onlooker consider becoming a Christian? We Christians seem no different from those around us.

Repeatedly, the Bible declares unity to be an important value, worth pouring our energies into and worth fighting for. Failure to preserve unity suggests an impotent God and affects the credibility of the gospel.

I am not advocating a "peace at any price" position. I am saying that in the West Christians have often fought for the wrong things and splintered groups over individual preferences and personalities rather than violations of the core of our biblical faith.

Paul's use of the body metaphor suggests that unless we work in harmony, we labor in vain. A fractured body is dysfunctional. Even more powerful is John's exhortation that Christians be one as the Trinity is one (Jn 17): unity is Godlike. Other passages suggest that disunity veils or hides the glory of God, while the glory of God is revealed through our living together in unity. The ability to respect human and cultural differences and not let them disrupt harmony is powerful testimony to the love and power of God.

Conflict, Unity and God's Glory

John 17 contains our Lord's prayer for those who were his disciples and those who would become his disciples. It could be called the "glory chapter," since *glory* or some variation of it occurs about nine times. The ultimate goal for our existence is to glorify God, and we are most like God when we are in union with one another just as the members of the Trinity are in union.

In the opening verses Jesus prays for himself, stating his concern for glorifying the Father. Next he turns his attention to the disciples and the glory they will bring to the Father. In his prayer for them he says, "I will remain in the world no longer, but they are still in the world, and I am coming to you. Holy Father, protect them by the power of your name" (v. 11). What kind of protection is Jesus requesting for the disciples? Is it physical protection because they will face persecution and martyrdom? Read further in verse 11: "so that they may be one as we are one." Jesus prays that their *unity* will be protected. This is a special kind of unity: "that they may be one as we are one." It is a unity that reflects the Godhead.

The oneness among Jesus' followers is to be modeled after that found in the Trinity. The Trinity is marked by diversity, distinct functions and roles, yet perfect unity. The disciples also have diversity, distinct functions (according to gifts and abilities) and varieties of roles to play, but they too are to be unified under the name of their Father and in their purpose of manifesting the glory of God. Jesus was quite aware that unity would be an ongoing struggle for his followers (see Lk 22:24-30).

In John 17:20 the Lord turns his thoughts toward us, his followers in the church today. "My prayer is not for them alone. I pray also for those who will believe in me through their message." Jesus makes a special request of the Father on our behalf. As he nears the moment of death, what does he consider most important for those who will carry his message and represent his glory on this earth? What is absolutely essential if the church is to be the "body of Christ" conveying the message of God's saving grace to the world? Jesus prays "that all of them may be one, Father, just as you are in me and I am in you. May they also be in us so that the world may believe that you have sent me" (v. 21).

Here, in one verse, is the link between the unity of God's people and the fulfillment of God's mission in this world. Our ability to resolve conflict, thus preserving unity, is directly related to people's coming to Christ. Humanly speaking, the world's believing is contingent on believers' oneness. The body of Christ, when its members live together in unity, becomes the visible manifestation of the triune God.

The contrary is also true. A lack of unity in our relationships veils the glory of God. So relationships affect mission. When we nurture unity among ourselves, we declare that God loves us and sent his Son to secure our redemption.

Why Doesn't God Send Revival?

Christians often say, "Why doesn't God send revival?" or "Why doesn't God give us some fruit for our labors?" Of course I do not have any final answer for that question, but John 17 suggests one reason could be that unresolved interpersonal conflicts have destroyed the unity that God uses to bring blessing and revival. Perhaps we need to pray for healing and restored relationships as well as revival. This text suggests that one is necessary for the other.

If the watching world observes the love of God holding believers together, they are confronted with the glory of God in his people. It is the glory of God that penetrates the darkness of their lives so that they are brought to a point of decision. But if they see broken relationships, schisms, gossip, and people exploiting one another, a message about God's power and love will have little effect. The glory of God and the impact of his gospel are tied to solidarity in his body.

The Priority of Relationships

The church at Corinth stood as dubious testimony to all that represented the worst of worldliness in the church. Whatever the problem, they had it in good measure. Only the most courageous pastor would consider accepting a call to this church. Suppose you had in front of you the long list of sins, problems and deficiencies in the Corinthian church. Now imagine that you were the apostle Paul and had been charged by God to write them a letter addressing the problems.

What topic would you address first? Idolatry? Abuse of the Lord's table? Divisiveness and schisms? Sexual immorality? Lawsuits against other believers? Fidelity and integrity in marriage? The flaunting of freedom before those whose consciences are weak? Personal rights? Improper uses of and attitudes about gifts? Impropriety in worship? Major theological errors? Poor stewardship of God's money?

Many of us would be inclined to start with the grosser sins, but Paul starts with an issue that he believes foundational to all others. In fact, he spends three chapters on this topic: building interpersonal solidarity. Unless relationships are intact, all other resolutions and corrections will be reduced to rubble as arguments, disagreements and disrespect continue. Unity is foundational to everything else that God wishes to accomplish in his church.

In 1:10 Paul begins with his goal: "I appeal to you, brothers, in the name of our Lord Jesus Christ, that all of you agree with one another so that there may be no divisions among you and that you may be perfectly united in mind and thought." He then mentions a report from Chloe's household that "there are quarrels among you."

"Quarrels" is the Greek word *schismata,* from which we get the

English word *schism*. This word was used in the garment industry to describe a piece of cloth that had somehow become mangled, torn, stained, wrinkled and altogether unattractive. Paul's hearers, coming across this word, would immediately think of the marketplace where the garment merchants hung their finest pieces to attract shoppers into their shops. No merchant would hang up a *schismata* garment, for the tears, holes, stains and wrinkles would only serve to drive customers away. Who would be interested in the merchandise if they saw *schismata?*

The Corinthians must have immediately gotten the point: who would be interested in considering Christ if when they saw Christians they saw *schismata?* Relationships affect the integrity of the gospel. Life and witness cannot be separated.

Realizing this, Paul begins dealing with the severe interpersonal problems. If *schismata* can be replaced with wholeness and unity, the power of the Gospel can be released.

In 1 Corinthians 3, divisiveness in the church is equated with spiritual infancy. It is ironic how often people think they are spiritually mature when they cause relational havoc in the church. Note that the contrast between "wood, hay or straw" and "gold, silver [and] costly stones" (3:12-15) is found in this context of interpersonal relationships. The gold, silver and costly stones should be seen as acts that contribute to harmony, affirmation, building one another up, thinking the best about the other, turning the other cheek, serving the body, esteeming the other greater than oneself. The wood, hay and straw may then be construed as attitudes and acts that disrupt unity for reasons God considers unworthy.

Paul closes his discourse on relationships with the analogy of the temple (3:16-17; compare 6:19-20). The word translated "temple" is the Old Testament word for "holy of holies" or "holiest place." The holiest place was the part of the temple where the visual presence of God's glory, called the *Shekinah* glory, could be seen. God no longer dwells in buildings, but in people by his Spirit. This indwelling makes each person and each gathering of God's people a holy place. In this text the emphasis rests on the local church body as the dwelling place of God, whereas in 6:19-20 the emphasis is on the individual as the holy place.[1]

Because God's habitation is in us, it follows that just as his glory was revealed in the temple, so his glory is seen in us—not the *Shekinah* glory, but the glory of God's presence in our unity, good works toward others, commitment to share his gospel and lives in obedience to his Word. In these ways we reveal his glory. But the text says that unity is one of the most important ways we reveal God's presence. Thus the destruction of unity is the destruction of something that God has made holy. Any activity contributing to disunity also contributes to the veiling of God's glory.

Of such importance is this concept that Paul issues a most ominous warning. Note 3:17: "If anyone destroys God's temple, God will destroy him; for God's temple is sacred, and you are that temple." God intends to build his people into one unified, harmonious, beautiful body that reveals the glory of God the Father, God the Son and God the Holy Spirit.

As a reminder of the Corinthians' history and need to remain vigilant in guarding relationships, Paul closes his second letter to the Corinthians with this exhortation: "Finally, brothers, good-by. Aim for perfection, listen to my appeal, be of one mind, live in peace. And the God of love and peace will be with you" (2 Cor 13:11).

Unity, God's Glory and Mission

In Romans 14 Paul deals with differences that endanger unity, primarily eating preferences and observance of special days. Rather than be divided over these matters and destroy each other (v. 15), he says, "accept him whose faith is weak, without passing judgment on disputable matters" (v. 1). "Disputable matters" refers to individual preferences, opinions or debatable points—issues where there is reasonable doubt as to the absolutely correct interpretation.

Therefore let us stop passing judgment on one another. Instead, make up your mind not to put any stumbling block or obstacle in your brother's way. (v. 13)

> Let us . . . make every effort to do what leads to peace and to mutual edification. Do not destroy the work of God for the sake of food. (vv. 19-20)

In this context of differences, Paul comes forth with a compelling plea for unity: "May the God who gives endurance and encouragement give you a spirit of unity among yourselves as you follow Christ Jesus, so that with one heart and mouth you may glorify the God and Father of our Lord Jesus Christ" (Rom 15:5-6).

It is noteworthy that Paul's plea for unity and oneness is joined with the notion of glorifying God. Paul then tells us how to make this unity a reality: "Accept one another, then, just as Christ accepted you" (15:7). "Accept" is another way of saying "honor" or "hold in high regard"—we are to treat each other as important, significant, worthy.

Christ is the model for our acceptance of each other. He treated us with honor even though we were undeserving and openly rebellious against him. In this way he reconciled many in eternal union with himself. And he delights when we daily express that union with him. Yet beyond our individual relationships with him, he yearns for the collective unity of his followers and their collective union with him.

A parent loves each child individually, but that love is heightened when the children love each other. When the children fight and become alienated, the parent's love remains, but the joy of that love is mingled with pain.

Paul explains that the natural outcome of unity is mission—"so that the Gentiles may glorify God for his mercy" (Rom 15:9). The glory of God revealed through the loving union of the people of God draws others into his mercy, so that they join their lives with ours in declaring his glory.

Summary

In most cultures of the world, friendships and community are among the strongest forces for bringing people to faith in Christ. If we are not good in relationships, if we cannot create solidarity, from a human standpoint there is little that will attract people to the gospel.

Building the unity of the body of Christ is the most effective way of jealously guarding the glory of God. Understanding and handling conflict with greater wisdom should minimize or prevent the damaging effects of broken relationships. It is a worthy goal to reduce the human suffering that accompanies alienation between people and groups. But even the healing motive is not sufficient to justify the pursuit of unity unless it is attached to unity's ultimate purpose: the revelation of God's glory.

3
HANDLING CONFLICT THE AMERICAN WAY

What I must do is all that
concerns me, not what people think.
RALPH WALDO EMERSON

Several years ago I conducted a workshop for about sixty North American mission executives. The theme was continuing education for missionaries. Two questions formed the core of the three days we had committed to the topic: "What are the most significant needs of field missionaries?" and "What can we do to assist in meeting those needs?"

When we were ready to identify the number-one need of overseas-based missionaries, the opinion was unanimous. Without any question or debate everyone concluded: the greatest problem among missionaries is relational breakdowns among themselves, and our greatest need is to help them deal with conflict by building positive interpersonal skills.

I was disappointed but not surprised. My experience suggested the same, but I had hoped that it was not typical.

What was true for missionaries seems to be true for North Americans in general. Increasingly the United States is becoming a nation of minorities where different frames of reference are producing alienation and violence. If the nation is to have a future that includes peace and prosperity, all of its peoples must not only coexist but learn to value, affirm and build upon each other's diversity. A healthy approach to understanding and managing conflict is a good beginning to cross-cultural relationships.

Conflict resolution has been explored by many researchers and writers in recent years, but most of their work has drawn from that of R. H. Thomas and K. W. Kilmann.[1] Thomas and Kilmann identified five ways most Westerners handle conflict, and I will summarize these strategies here.

The Win-Lose Strategy

Win-lose people assume that everything should be seen as right or wrong. They have a very small "gray" area and tend not to be very flexible or willing to negotiate. Everything must be judged as right or wrong, even obvious differences; thus it follows that everything that is "like me" will be judged as right and everything "unlike me" will be judged as wrong. Such people have little tolerance for ambiguity. Right and wrong must be determined as quickly as possible so one knows how to treat the matter or the person. If what was said or done is "wrong," corrective action is required. If it is "right," affirmation and encouragement are in order.

Perhaps the best illustration of a person who takes the win-lose position is the TV personality Archie Bunker of the 1970s series *All in the Family*. People all over the world have heard of Archie Bunker. Furthermore, everyone knows "Archie Bunkers" in their own network of relationships—the people who need to be right on every issue, who find it difficult to admit they were wrong, who find it hard to value differences, much less celebrate them, who try to get everyone to conform to their way of seeing things.

Win-lose people assume there is only one right position on most matters, so they competitively attempt to win others over to their position. The win-lose person employs a variety of tactics in trying to convert others from the error of their ways:

□ physical force—make the other person comply

□ threats—threaten loss of reward, loss of relationship or punishment

□ intimidation—try to frighten the other person into agreement

□ silence—refuse to speak until the other person gives in

□ verbiage and volume—outtalk or outshout the other person

□ point out past failures—say, "Because you were wrong in another situation, you are wrong now"

□ pull rank—"I am your boss [father, professor, supervisor]"

□ reward—promise something of value if they give in

□ spiritual one-upmanship—say, "While I was praying and reading the Bible, God gave me this conviction"; imply that God is on their side

The win-lose person is highly competitive and seeks to win whenever there is a difference of opinion. This is especially true if the person has personal or positional power. People who have a high need to win all debates or arguments are usually willing to sacrifice relationships in order to get their way. They tend to be quite assertive, especially if challenged, and will fight for everything as though all things were of equal value. They seem unable to distinguish between major and minor issues and usually do not know when to just "let it go."

Win-lose people usually fail to see themselves in this category. Others, however, see it quite clearly. If such a person is to be successfully confronted, usually several people need to approach him or her together. Going one-on-one with the win-lose person generally is not productive; the encounter becomes little more than an argument.

Someone has said, "Maturity is knowing more and more what is worth fighting for and what is not worth fighting for." The person who has a need to win at every point needs to ponder this definition of maturity.

Of course, we must not go to the extreme of assuming that winning in a relationship is always bad. Sometimes we should strive for a win position. I tell my students, for example, that if someone suggests you engage in premarital sex, your virginity is worth fighting for; take a win position and be willing to sacrifice the relationship if it must come to that. That is one conflict you do not want to lose.

If someone says to me, "Would you like to have an open-minded discussion on the resurrection of Christ?" my answer is no. I am not open-minded on that point and will only take a win position if I get into a discussion about it.

There are certain goals, beliefs, values or ideals that you do not want to compromise or sacrifice, and it is wise to know in advance what those are. Let them be guided by Scripture. Be dogmatic and stubborn where God is, and be flexible where he is.

The win-lose style of handling conflict has significant implications in cross-cultural situations. We shall return to it later.

Avoidance
The person who tries to manage conflict by avoiding it believes that differences are bad, they always cause hard feelings and broken relationships, and no good can come from confronting conflict.

Yet avoiding conflict or withdrawing from it does not allow these people to preserve important goals, values and ideals—nor does it allow them to preserve relationships. They lose on both counts and end up with weak or superficial relationships and little or no influence on important decisions.

Larry sensed that God was calling him to the mission field. Part of his training included an internship in a church. During the sixth month of his training, Larry mentioned to me that there seemed to be a little misunderstanding with his pastor. He was feeling uncomfortable but did not know what to do. He was not sure if the pastor sensed it as well and, if so, how he was feeling about it. I suggested that it was probably a small issue and a talk with the pastor would easily set everything right. Larry pondered my advice without making a commitment.

About a month later Larry brought the issue up again. This time he was clearly anxious and distraught. The problem had not really become bigger except in Larry's mind as he struggled with going to the pastor. I urged Larry to speak with the pastor; I even suggested words he might use to introduce the problem as he perceived it. I assured him the issue was not that serious and the pastor would surely understand. A happy resolution would come easily, but he must not continue delaying. Larry agreed but did not evidence much confidence or enthusiasm.

Shortly thereafter the pastor called me, wondering if I knew why Larry was acting rather unusual. The pastor had asked Larry if anything was wrong, but Larry had simply said everything was all right. Since I had some authority over Larry, I decided to brief the pastor on the situation in the hope of facilitating a speedy and positive resolution. We agreed to give Larry a few more days before the pastor gently took the initiative.

Larry had done a good job and earned everyone's respect, and we all saw him as a friend. We looked forward to getting the situation cleared up, since there were only two months left in Larry's internship.

Not long after my conversation with the pastor, my telephone rang. It was the pastor. In a confused voice he asked me if I knew where Larry was. He had found a note from Larry saying that he did not want to be a missionary any longer and therefore saw no reason to continue his internship. His room was cleaned out. No one in that church saw or heard from Larry again.

I had telephone numbers for his parents and his home church, so I called immediately. Yes, he had returned, they said, but he refused to talk to anyone about the situation other than to say that he had decided against being a missionary and wanted to get on with life.

Larry had responded to conflict with avoidance; when he was unable to share his feelings, he decided to withdraw physically and emotionally. Thus he gave up his goal of being a missionary and also lost the respect of the church members. Personal values as well as relationships were forfeited because Larry had only one way to handle conflict.

Tom, a missionary, had a similar problem. Everyone liked Tom because he was quiet and seemed willing to do things that others resisted—such as taking responsibility for the high-school young people during annual conference when all the missionaries and their families would gather to fellowship and conduct business. While the missionaries met, someone had to care for the children and teenagers. Most wanted to be in the meetings; so finding someone to care for the children for the bulk of the day was a bit of a problem—except for the high-schoolers, who had a ready volunteer in Tom. With his wife, Tom would plan delightful activities. His willingness to serve was much appreciated.

One day I told him how fortunate the missionaries were to have someone like him. He seemed embarrassed that someone would see him as valuable. Then I summarized a rather hotly debated controversy that had broken out during the missionary meetings that day. Since Tom had been out with the teenagers, I thought he would appreciate a summary. When I asked him what he thought, I heard a series of evasive remarks that suggested Tom was unwilling to take a position.

"I wasn't here to listen to the discussion, so I really couldn't say one way or another" was his first response. "It is a rather complicated matter, and both sides seem to have a good argument, so it all depends upon how you look at it," he said as I probed further.

"But how do you see it?" I asked, pushing the point.

"Well, I need to give it more thought; but right now I need to meet my family to get ready for the evening meal," he answered, walking away.

Tom's expertise at avoiding conflict was evident. While he was a good listener, he never took a position on anything of importance.

Both Larry and Tom took the avoidance or withdrawing approach to potential conflict situations. Consequently, neither had influence in terms of policies and directions, and their relationships tended to be quite shallow.

There are times when avoiding conflict or withdrawing from it is a good idea. Obviously, if the problem is trivial and not worth time and energy, it may be wise just to avoid it. I find this is important for parents to remember. They tend to treat every issue as life and death and try to steer the child in the "right" direction. When the issue is relatively unimportant, I tell them, let the child decide and begin to make the important discovery that each decision has consequences.

Strategic withdrawal can be a very wise choice. Perhaps emotions have been running high, and if you confront you may act unwisely or lose control. In such situations, avoid the conflict for a short period of time until you cool off and can reenter the situation creatively and with emotions under control.

You may also wish to avoid conflict if the potential consequences are too serious. For about a year I regularly ministered on the streets of Chicago in the evenings. If I saw a group of people coming toward me and there was the potential of hostility, I carefully avoided conflict by crossing the street well ahead of their arrival. I did not know what a confrontation with one of these groups might bring, but clearly it made sense to avoid danger.

Avoiding conflict can be a sign of wisdom and maturity, but it can also signal an unwillingness to discuss important issues or a refusal to take a stand on a significant decision.

Giving In
Many people face conflict situations and simply give in, accommodate or smooth over the differences. Sometimes this response is called yielding. These people see most things as negotiable. Differences are rarely worth fighting about, so they find ways of accommodating to the other party. Maintaining relationships is most important, and someone must make the sacrifice of giving in or people would always be fighting. Nothing is accomplished by disagreement.

People who exercise the give-in approach to conflict resolution use phrases like

☐ "I can see your point. Maybe there is something to it."

☐ "Since you feel strongly, I am not going to disagree."

☐ "It really doesn't matter that much. It will all come out in the wash."

☐ "They didn't mean anything by it. Just ignore it."

☐ "Sometimes you just have to take a few bumps and forget it."

☐ "I think I can give in, just this once."

☐ "Let it pass. It isn't worth making a fuss about."

While these people enjoy great relationships, they often forfeit personal goals and values. They can easily be taken advantage of, since they have difficulty saying no. Being people-pleasers, they are often doing things for others in the hope of averting any conflict or of softening some conflict.

Edith Bunker of *All in the Family* usually took this approach with her win-lose husband, Archie. Always eager to please, Edith would scurry around doing things for Archie and rarely raised a dissenting voice. She good-naturedly gave everyone the benefit of a doubt and assumed the best about others. When Archie and his son-in-law would get into heated debate, it was Edith who felt the pain and sometimes shouted, "Stop arguing!" The tactic usually brought silence but rarely peace.

In fairness to Edith, there were a few times when she refused to back down and with impassioned feeling blurted out, "No, Archie, you're wrong!" The person who generally gives in can be pushed too far and will then strike back with a nonnegotiable win position.

When is it wise to give in? If the issue is of little consequence, it can make sense to let others have their way, especially if maintaining the relationship is of greater importance than winning the conflict. Save your time and energy for more important issues. Then, if you are wrong, it is wise to say, "I am sorry. I was wrong. You were right." Many people find this difficult to do, but it is very important for preserving the relationship. Also, there is nothing wrong with giving in this time so that next time your preference might be honored. This is a worthwhile approach when minor differences occur. For example: "Tonight I will go with you to the concert if next weekend you will go with me to the museum."

You may occasionally want to let others have their own way so that they might learn their mistake through suffering the consequences. Obviously you wouldn't want to give in if the potential consequences were too serious. But let's assume the consequences are not too serious. For example, my college-age son wanted to buy a fourteen-year-old, 124,000-mile junker of a car. He had an affection for it which fell somewhere between pity and respect for the aged. I confess, it did seem to run well. Sensing his attachment to the rickety thing, I did not let him know that I would not have bought it, because I did not want to contradict his feelings. We discussed the pros and cons, but the decision was his. Even if he bought it and his decision turned out to be a mistake, the consequences would not be severe. The loss of a relatively small amount of money would be totally insignificant in the larger context of his whole life. For me, avoiding potential conflict or hurt feelings seemed the wisest response. And my son eventually decided against buying the car.

Compromise

The compromising person believes that it is impossible to have everything, so everyone should give a little and get a little. Sometimes you may get a little less, other times a little more, but it will all even out over time. Life is the art of negotiating to some happy middle ground.

Compromise is common in labor-management negotiations. Each party comes with demands that appear outrageous to the other party. No one gets upset, though, because everyone knows that many of these will fall by the wayside before the final settlement is reached. It is assumed that taking an extreme position at first is the best way to bargain, that eventually the parties will settle on a happy medium, with neither side getting everything it had originally asked for, and that everyone will be basically satisfied. "Life is a series of tradeoffs," reasons the person who uses compromise as a way of managing conflict.

On the surface this seems a very desirable way to handle conflict situations. Everybody comes away happy (at least in theory). Actually, though, this method means that one or both parties must give up something, and it may be something important. Then one party will walk away dissatisfied and unhappy. Members of that group may subsequently look for ways to "even the score" and thus sabotage the agreement. Or next time they may take a win-lose position. So there are two major problems with compromise: it endangers the relationship, and each side must be vigilant in order not to compromise something important.

Another problem with compromise is that it works poorly when either party has disproportionate power. If one party has greater power, she or he can negotiate tougher, from a position of superior strength, knowing that the other party cannot bargain as an equal. Again, one side is likely to walk away unhappy.

Like the other styles of handling conflict, compromise is neither bad nor good in itself. Its value depends on how it is applied and in what situations. We don't want to compromise on important goals or values, but if certain goals or hopes are only moderately important to us, it may make sense to give them up in order to achieve something else.

Compromise may be necessary or desirable in an emergency or when time is a critical factor. If a crisis is looming and a decision is hard to reach, compromise may be the most desirable option. If a compromise cannot be reached, all may be lost. As in other situations, before making the decision we must weigh the values and goals that would need to be compromised. What values and goals do you refuse to compromise under any circumstances? What might you compromise under certain circumstances? It is helpful to think about this in advance.

Carefronting
"Carefronting" means directly approaching the other person in a caring way so that achieving a win-win solution is most likely. With this

approach neither party loses anything important and the relationship does not suffer. However, several conditions must be met to achieve a mutual win situation through carefronting.

1. The two parties can come together, meet face to face and talk with open honesty.

2. They each make a commitment to preserve the relationship and dispassionately explain the values/goals that each wishes to protect or achieve.

3. They can creatively find a solution in which they can both be equal winners, with neither giving up anything of value, and thus preserve the relationship.

4. They can do this with reason, keeping emotions under control.

5. They are both able to separate the person from the issue and speak objectively to that end.

6. Neither will be satisfied with a solution until the other is also completely at peace with it.

Striving for the win-win solution has been the focus of many management and interpersonal relationship books in recent years, and rightly so. It is a major step in breaking the competitive nature of problem-solving and replacing it with cooperative attitudes and skills.[2]

Some authors argue that carefronting is not simply one way of handling conflict but the only right way.[3] They cite Matthew 18:15-17:

If your brother sins against you, go and show him his fault, just between the two of you. If he listens to you, you have won your brother over. But if he will not listen, take one or two others along, so that "every matter may be established by the testimony of two or three witnesses." If he refuses to listen to them, tell it to the church; and if he refuses to listen even to the church, treat him as you would a pagan or a tax collector.

The text seems clear that direct, face-to face confrontation in a caring, loving way is the biblical approach to conflict. What is not so clear is whether this is intended to be the *only* approach to conflict or whether it represents one good approach. We must also ask whether this approach is, at least to some extent, more acceptable in some cultures than in others. Cultural variables may dictate how to approach conflict and help us see some Scriptures in a new light. How culture affects our style of conflict resolution is the theme of the following chapters.

Summary

It's important to know each of the five styles of conflict resolution—and to notice which particular style(s) one is prone to use. Knowing that we have a choice helps us choose the best option for a given situation. If we are locked into one or two options, we run the risk of aggravating the conflict and putting stress on the relationship. Being aware of the range of choices, we can choose an approach that will help us preserve goodwill without sacrificing other things that we value.

In this chapter we have been looking at *Western* ways of resolving conflict. Do other cultures use different styles of conflict management? If so, why? What cultural values support other ways of handling conflict? Do these styles find biblical support?

4

CONFLICT
AND CULTURAL
VALUES

Do not remove a fly
from your neighbor's face with a hatchet
CHINESE PROVERB

A few Westerners along with several Asians formed a team of workers in an Asian country. Charged with a special high-pressure project and rigid deadlines, workers began to feel the stress. It was increasingly evident that one person in the office was not living up to expectations and not fulfilling the job description. Everyone felt the person had the ability but was not putting forth the effort.

Tension increased, taxing people's patience and putting stress on the all-important cooperative relationships. The project director, an Asian, called the team together and accused them of poor performance, lacking in motivation and endangering the success of the project. The conclusion of the speech went something like this: "We must work harder; we must work together; we must be successful in this project."

Some Westerners felt misjudged, angry and misunderstood. Why should they be faulted when everyone knew that only one person constituted the problem? Why not take that person aside and deal with the problem individually? Why should everyone be blamed?

While the Westerners murmured their confusion and nursed their hurt feelings, the Asian team members returned to their work quite unruffled. Almost immediately a change was evident around the office, including a better level of performance by the problem person.

In many cultures of the world, individuals are not singled out and identified as being responsible for a problem. Such singling out would almost certainly cause the person to leave the company, and repercussions would be felt even in community relations. Rather, problems are seen as a communal affair. The manager was, in fact, reprimanding the individual but in an indirect way. A group reprimand was also in order because the whole group was in some measure responsible for not bringing the person up to acceptable standards. By distancing themselves from the person, the other team members were contributing to the problem.

Conflict and Directness

Westerners have treated the five styles of handling conflict (outlined in chapter three) as though they were universal. If, as many Christians have argued, the carefronting approach is the only biblical approach, it must be applied across cultures. But this could be unwise. I suggest the Bible supports several means of handling conflict in addition to those used in Western cultures. If we are aware of the alternatives, we can be more culturally sensitive in handling conflict. This will enable us to share biblical principles without imposing Western culture on other people.

The carefronting approach works best in a culture that values a direct, confrontational, one-on-one approach. Most Western cultures fall into this category. Language in North America supports directness. For example, consider some the following expressions:

☐ Tell it like it is.

☐ Don't beat around the bush.

□ Put your cards on the table.
□ Give it to me straight.
□ Be up-front with me.
□ Lay it on the line.
□ Level with me.
□ Straight from the horse's mouth.

These idioms reveal something about the Western world. They tell us that we like straight, clear and direct communication. We do not like it if someone speaks to us in obscure, oblique or circuitous ways. This we judge to be devious, deceptive, evasive, even sinister. So if someone is not straightforward with us, we immediately become suspicious and impute to that person some negative intention or motivation, as though he or she were hiding something or trying to avoid the truth. Such behavior leads us to assume guilt.

Directness does have some distinct advantages. One, speaking to each other face to face should decrease the possibility of misunderstanding. Two, those who work problems out together often find that their relational bond is strengthened. Three, being open and direct with one another is more time-efficient. Issues are handled quickly so both parties can move on to other things. Western culture places considerable value on these advantages.

The Active Voice
Even Western grammar encourages directness. The English language relies heavily on the active voice. The active voice provides the most precision by pointing to a particular person or thing. It allows us to specify who is responsible and thus deserving of blame or reward and honor. For example, I may ask members of my family, "Who forgot to turn out the lights?" or "Did you track mud onto the carpet?" If something goes wrong, we can determine who is responsible, make sure the individual knows it and take steps to keep it from happening again. The active voice reduces ambiguity and uncertainty because it designates,

specifies, points out and seeks accuracy.

Placing blame is a very natural, even unconscious social activity for many of us in Western culture. We do it in the interest of improvement, to show people what they did wrong or how they might do something better. Of course we assume that everyone wants to be told what she or he did wrong and how to do things better. And we are quite surprised when others seem offended by our good intentions.

Yet this same directness, so little noticed in the West, would in most of the world be considered rude and immature. Such directness strains, even ruptures, relationships and certainly disrupts harmony. The direct person, especially in conflict situations, risks personal credibility and is seen as untrustworthy.

Westerners also use the active voice to honor and praise: "My son won academic honors" or "My daughter is first chair in the orchestra." Again, the active verb indicates exactly who is doing what. Little room is left for ambiguity.

Using the active voice to praise someone in another culture seems like a good idea. In many places it is, but in some cultures you can cause embarrassment by giving such direct praise. Singling out one individual for praise while failing to recognize the "supporting cast" without whom any success would have been impossible is viewed as myopic and ill-mannered at best, contemptuous at worst.

This is especially true in Japan where a strong group orientation exists. The Japanese have a proverb, "The nail that sticks up will get pounded down," meaning that no one is singled out for praise, because any success should be recognized as a group effort. Whatever success one person has would not have been possible without the support of others. So if I single out someone for praise, I have violated group effort and harmony.

Even in indirect cultures, though, there are times when directness is acceptable. One may be direct if every effort has been made to solve the problem through indirect means. Because indirectness is intentionally vague, the other party may fail to catch the point. In such cases directness is warranted. Or one may be justified in using directness when the other party understands the indirect messages but refuses to respond appropriately.

Finally, directness is often acceptable when one becomes an insider in the other culture. Sometimes this is referred to as becoming a member of the "in-group." An in-group can be an extended family, a group of business colleagues, a social club or another social or religious grouping, perhaps even an athletic team. Here directness is acceptable because the trust bond is so strong that everything is tightly protected within the ranks. That is, no one fears that this information is going to cause anyone embarrassment, and no one fears that praise will elevate anyone to an inappropriate position. There is a tacit understanding that each member protects the others from any public disgrace.

The "outsider" is someone outside the in-group, including everyone from outside the culture—the missionary, businessperson, tourist and so on. The outsider must work hard to earn in-group status and many never achieve it. The one who does become an insider wins the privilege to be direct at certain times.

An Underlying but Powerful Assumption

Directness in language implies that one can speak to a *problem* without offending the *person*. Western culture tends to separate the person from the problem, the person from the action or the person from the idea. Thus Westerners feel free to criticize ideas, behaviors and failures of others. Usually such criticism is prefaced by "I have nothing against you personally, but . . ." or "I say this to you as a friend." Even many Westerners cringe upon hearing such words, because the distinction between the person and the idea or behavior is not very precise.

Our schooling has encouraged us to evaluate and critique one another's ideas. The smart person can discern inconsistencies in another person's idea or argument, point them out and win the teacher's approval by destroying the other person's idea. Such a person receives

honor and praise. Logic and truth reign supreme in the classroom—
sometimes at the cost of human dignity.

In cultures where harmony, solidarity and group cohesion are primary
values, no such distinction exists. The person and the idea are one. To
criticize my idea, behavior, or words is to criticize me as a person. Carl
Becker cites Confucius on the idea of *hsin* as an example of this
continuity between the person and behavior:

> Words are not to be treated as sounds, ideas, or propositions which
> exist independently of their utterers, to be judged by critical linguistic
> analysis. They are inextricably interrelated to the person who utters
> them. Their truth depends on his character, and his truth depends on
> the character of his words. Thus, it becomes impossible to scrutinize
> or criticize an idea without casting aspersions on the character of the
> person who voices it. Since one of our primary duties is to be
> respectful to men (Analects, XIV, 29) then we should sooner allow
> their mistakes to pass uncriticized than exhibit a lack of proper respect
> for their words and hence their selves.[1]

The inseparability of the person and the behavior has a powerful effect
on how relationships are conducted in non-Western cultures. One of the
effects is indirectness.

Culture and Indirectness

Most people in the world do not place a high value on direct, face-to-face
confrontation to solve a conflict. Such directness is considered crude,
harsh, uncultured and certainly disrespectful if not cruel. Asian cultures
possess this attitude most strongly, but African and Latin American
cultures also demonstrate this view. These cultures prefer to approach
conflict indirectly, circuitously, obliquely. So language is neither direct
nor pointed. The passive and stative voices are most prominent. The
passive voice suggests that someone was acted upon and was not an
active participant. The stative voice simply describes what is or what was
without any indication of who was responsible. Neither voice supplies

precision as to the subject, the actor. Neither voice carries the function of pointing to a person. Therefore, no specific person is blamed or held responsible for a problem. The problem simply exists.

The use of the passive and stative voices serves to protect "face," a person's honor. For example, a statement as simple as "I forgot" is rendered in Spanish as "Se me olvidó," meaning literally "It forgot itself to me." When I say "I forgot" (active voice), I identify myself as the responsible agent. But that could be embarrassing and cause me to lose face or be shamed. Thus the passive voice is used, suggesting that it happened to me but not implying direct responsibility. And, my face is protected. For example, consider how a given comment might be stated by a Westerner and someone from the Two-Thirds World:

Westerners Tend to Say	Two-Thirds World People Tend to Say
I broke the plate.	The plate fell and broke.
I missed the bus.	The bus left without me.
We have a problem; let's talk about it.	A problem exists; we must hope it goes away.
I forgot to check the oil in the lawnmower and burned out the engine.	The lawnmower does not work. It needs to get fixed.
My Walkman was stolen.	My Walkman has become lost.
I forgot.	It forgot itself to me.
I was in an accident.	An accident happened to me; or, My car was damaged.

Understandably, passive and stative voices allow for considerable ambiguity and sometimes, quite honestly, confusion. Perhaps this is why many Westerners struggle so much in learning another language. It may be even more difficult to interpret the language after we have learned it. How would you interpret the following story, which I draw from Marvin Mayers, if you would had been there?

A mother and her son have been visiting friends, and find that it is too late to get transportation back to their province. So within hearing of her friends, she comments to her son, "Son, we are very poor. We cannot go back to the province today. Maybe we have to stay here in town."[2]

Did you react the way I did? I wondered why she did not ask her friends outright. Why did she speak to her son?

The woman is hoping to stay with her friends, but to ask directly would make her look bad, as though she had not planned adequately. Furthermore, it would put her friends in a position of shame if for some reason they cannot accommodate her and her son. As it happened, though, the friends immediately realized she did not have any money to stay in a hotel and asked her to stay with them for the night.

Western Misinterpretations

When an indirect method of handling conflict is used, the Westerner often misinterprets this as (1) lack of courage to confront the person, (2) unwillingness to deal with the issue, (3) lack of commitment to solve the problem or (4) refusal to take responsibility for one's actions. In fact, the person may be displaying both courage and commitment, but in ways that are not understood by those of us who come from a culture that values directness.

Let me illustrate. Eunice, a black South African, was employed to help my wife care for the house and the children. Eunice worked hard and was trustworthy. We were delighted she was with us.

One day she had just cleared the table of some dishes when I heard a crash in the kitchen. With a voice that I hoped conveyed nonjudgmental inquiry, I asked, "Eunice, did you break a dish?" I even raised my voice just a touch at the end to be sure not to communicate anger or disgust.

Note my use of the active voice. I even called her by name so there would be no mistaking who I believed had broken the dish. I had no malice toward Eunice, and I certainly did not intend to convey disrespect; this is the way everyone spoke where I grew up. It was so very natural. Wasn't everyone like me?

"No, Umfundise [term of respect]. The cup fell and it died."

I thought, "What do you mean, 'the cup fell and died?' What kind of answer is that?" Unhappy with her response and wanting some indication of accountability, I pursued the point.

"You mean that you dropped the cup?" Again I tried to use a tone that would show my desire to clarify. I was looking for a simple admission of guilt but was not even aware why that should be important. It was just the way things should be done.

"The dish fell and died," she said a second time with a more subdued voice, this time dropping the term of respect.

Still confused by her answer but thinking that yet another attempt to get "the real story" would probably be unproductive, I decided to drop the issue. *Why can't she just give a straight answer?* was the frustrating thought that lodged in my mind.

Her use of the stative voice ("The cup fell and it died") struck me as evasive. *Why isn't she willing to assume responsibility for her actions? She's an adult. Being willing to accept blame is a mature adult behavior. What is her problem?* I wondered, believing that my confusion had been produced by some deficiency on her part.

In essence I was wishing Eunice would be more Western, more like me, so I would not be forced outside of my comfort zone. If I could change her, I could avoid the awkwardness of changing myself.

When I resist change, I wallow in my myopic ignorance, forfeiting the joy of learning from others and the exhilaration of discovering that God's world far exceeds my experience. When I resist change I remain firmly anchored in egocentrism, mistakenly believing that my cultural patterns are the best and only way. Ultimately this arrogance leads others to conclude that Christ and his gospel are simply a variation of Western culture.

To understand Eunice's response, we have to probe further into cultural values. Why was she indirect? What made it so difficult for her to accept responsibility for so simple a problem? For answers we must look at the values of shame, honor and face.

Shame, Honor and Face

Central values in many of the cultures in the Two-Thirds World are "saving face," "not causing another to feel shame" and "maintaining honor." While there are technical distinctions among these concepts, here I will treat them as basically synonymous and interchangeable. Keep in mind, then, that the notion of "honor" in Japan will be similar to the concept of "shame" in the Philippines and "saving face" in Thailand.

These values serve several important purposes: preserving smooth interpersonal relationships, maintaining harmony, minimizing potential conflict, restoring of community solidarity (family, tribal or group) and facilitating communication between the various levels of society. George Foster summarizes the differences in handling conflict and the relationship to shame, honor and face:

> Prevailing concepts about how to settle conflict are quite distinct from those of the United States, but they conform well to the realities of life in the village, and in many respects they are highly humane. The basic principle of conflict resolution reflects the principle of equilibrium which underlies all feeling about the healthy social organism: maintain the status quo at all costs; don't humble or shame others, but protect your rights.[3]

In a shame culture the worst thing one person can do is cause another to be shamed, lose face or be dishonored. C. H. Dodd says that in Asian cultures "shame is the worst thing that can happen to a person, next to losing one's group identity. In traditional Japanese culture, disgrace potential is an important decision-making characteristic. If a policy or a person has the potential for bringing about shame, or loss of face, then such risks are not likely to be sought."[4]

It is considered an even greater tragedy if this shaming is done in public. To be shamed or lose face before one's family, friends or esteemed colleagues is to be avoided at all costs. The person who shames another publicly seriously violates standard social protocol and endangers the harmonious equilibrium of the relationship. Strained or broken relationships are virtually inevitable.

In the Thai language, one word for causing someone shame means literally "to tear one's face off"—causing someone to appear ugly before others. The English words *humiliation* and *disgrace* may come closest to the concept of shame, but they fail to carry the intense negative impact and social stigma of shame in these Two-Thirds World cultures.

Shame, loss of face and dishonor may occur in a variety of ways. One may dishonor oneself by not living up to certain goals. For example, the Japanese student who is denied entry into the preferred university experiences great dishonor and, in extreme cases, may commit suicide as a means of restoring family honor. One might be shamed by the actions of a family member; in Arab society, especially Muslim, to become a Christian is to shame the family and the Islamic religion. The shamed family tries to restore honor and face by excommunicating the Christian convert and treating the person as though he or she were dead or never existed. If the family wishes to restore itself from extreme shame, it may physically punish the departed member, sometimes threatening or even taking the person's life.

One may cause shame by suggesting that the other party is responsible for a problem or difficulty that exists. Or a sense of shame may occur if expectations were not fulfilled. Eunice felt shame because I indicated she had done something wrong: she failed to meet my expectations of handling the dishes without breaking them. The petrol attendants (the gas-station workers who gave me inaccurate directions) would feel shame if someone needed their help and they were unable to provide it. To cover or avoid the shame, Eunice used the passive and stative voices, and the petrol attendant gave me well-intentioned but misdirected help.

One may also create shame by causing a person to be out of solidarity with the group or causing a minority to be out of harmony with the majority. The concept of majority rule, so common in the Western world, illustrates this. In a one-person-one-vote system the majority prevails or wins and the minority loses. In the West if one has voted but still loses to the majority, it is counted unfortunate but usually not considered a tragedy. One simply determines to work harder to change the outcome in the next election. In the meantime one makes the best of it and tries to support the majority as much as possible.

But whenever there are winners there are also losers. In the Two-Thirds World, losers often suffer loss of face, a sense of shame at being affiliated with losing. So in many instances people will find out how others are voting and will vote with the majority to avoid loss of face, even though they may be voting contrary to their better judgment.

Those who vote their conscience and end up among the losing minority may suffer shame and loss of honor. To restore some of the lost honor, they may resort to a variety of strategies. The most common way is to break off from the majority and start a new group with as many of the minority people as possible. Others, rather than break away, will attempt some sort of revenge, such as spreading rumors or other subversive activities that make it difficult for the majority to conduct business. Of course they would deny such activity if ever confronted. In more extreme cases the "loser" may isolate himself or herself, go into exile for a time or retreat to the ultimate isolation of suicide.[5] This would be very unlike the tactic of former U.S. president Jimmy Carter, who plunged into public service after his landslide loss in his bid for reelection.

These various reactions to losing happen with less frequency and with less intensity as Western ways become more prevalent and are better understood. Nonetheless, the traditional strategies for restoring honor continue to be very strong in rural areas of the Two-Thirds World and relatively prominent in metropolitan centers.

Problems with the Majority-Rule System

The majority-rule system pits people and groups against each other. In the West, where individualism prevails and losing is regrettable but not shameful, majority rule is an efficient and often effective way of making decisions. But in the Two-Thirds World, where collectivism (acting as a group in solidarity) is preferred to individualism, the majority-rule procedure is seen as schismatic and disruptive of harmony. As I noted above, to avoid the shame of being in the minority, people will often determine which way the vote is going and simply join in. Although the vote is unanimous, or virtually so, disappointment soon sets in because so many people seem uncommitted to the decision. Westerners cannot understand how people could vote for something and then not get involved in the implementation process.

Perhaps a Western leader has a high profile in the group and has made known his or her wishes regarding a forthcoming vote on some issue. The people, wishing not to cause this person shame, may comply by unanimous approval but then show halfhearted support in follow-through. The Westerner's early enthusiasm will quickly be replaced by confusion as the people's lack of support is discovered. Then the Westerner begins to question the people's sincerity, integrity, even maturity, resulting in mistrust.

The Westerner could have avoided the problem by refusing to make any strong statement about how he or she hoped the vote might go. Often a generic statement like "We must vote in a way that will benefit the people and reflect Christian values" allows everyone to vote their conscience. But being unaware of the shame factor in this culture, the Westerner did not realize that the people felt pressured to vote a certain way to keep the leader from suffering the shame of defeat. From the people's cultural frame of reference, they were acting graciously by protecting the Westerner. The Westerner, misinterpreting the situation, begins to attribute negative characteristics to the people. Out of such simple misunderstandings grow the seeds of conflict.

Rival Factions

A most difficult situation occurs when two rival groups exist in proximity to each other. The Westerner (missionary, businessperson, community development worker or student) must know the relationship between the two groups (whether villages, tribes, barrios, clans or districts), or things could become problematic.

Offering a program, or even offering friendship, to one village before it is offered to the other may not only alienate the latter but also keep them from ever considering such a program, even though it could greatly benefit them. Hostilities directed toward one group are transferred to all who align themselves with that group. When these perceptions are fixed in the people's minds—and it matters little if they are valid—the implications are immediate and pervasive.

Mary Hollnsteiner offers one example: "Opposing factions will attack almost any project sponsored by their rivals, finding innumerable reasons why it is bad for the community. Though the project may have the noblest aims, such as improving the health of the children, the other side will surely find something in it to criticize. Every resident knows the real reason for the attack: the enmity between the factions involved."[6]

George Foster observes, "Establishing friendship with a person identifies the outsider with that person's group or faction, and by implication, he assumes the villagers' hostility to rival groups and factions."[7] To be effective with two or more groups who have some animosity among them, then, the outsider must take great care to be seen as impartial. But it seems unlikely that such a stance will be perceived as nonpartisan by all the groups over time. Some group is likely to perceive favoritism in some direction, real or imagined. Unwittingly, one can easily intensify historic divisions.

Here are some guidelines for involvement in multiple groups, whether you are doing evangelism, church planting, business or community development projects.

1. Know the groups with whom you intend to work. What has been the history of their relationships? What is the present status of their relationship? Are there any issues smoldering beneath the surface that have explosive potential? Do the two groups share similar customs, economic status, religious beliefs, degree of progressiveness?

2. Assuming you are satisfied that you can work with both groups, lay

the foundation by meeting with leadership from both groups at the same time. If you meet with the leader(s) from one group first, that could be perceived as favoritism and sabotage the effort from the beginning.

3. As far as possible, keep time and budget commitments equally divided between the two groups. This may require the keeping of records showing hours and finances expended.

4. Maintain regular joint meetings with the leadership. Be sensitive to subtle, indirect messages that may suggest one party is feeling disgruntled about something. Pursue any perceived inequities in private or in some indirect way (I will suggest various indirect strategies later).

In the final analysis, the gospel of Christ becomes the only firm basis for reconciliation between hostile groups. But until such a foundation is laid, we must be culturally sensitive and avoid stirring up rivalries.[8]

Vested Interests

Whenever vested interests are involved, relationships become critical for creating or resolving conflict. Religious leaders understandably see Christianity as a threat to their vocation and status in the community. Christianity may also be seen as a threat to the world and life view the people have held for centuries. Similarly, local moneylenders see the loan banks set up by external community-development workers as a threat to their income, jeopardizing the well-being of spouse, children and future. Traditional healers see the new hospital or clinic as usurping their authority and traditional role in society. All these people face disgrace, humiliation and the strong possibility of becoming outcasts, nonpersons shunned by friends and family.

Everyone has some vested interest, and conflict often focuses exactly at that point. The outsider who gains early awareness and understanding of such interests can creatively manage the situation so that dignity is protected. Protecting people's dignity not only protects them from losing face but preserves an openness and trust in the relationship that the Spirit of God can use to glorify the Father. An excellent illustration of this is offered by Bruce Olson in *Bruchko*.

Olson tells of a pinkeye epidemic among the Motilones, a tribal group of Indians in a remote jungle region of Colombia. Pinkeye is not life-threatening, but the infection can lead to more serious problems. The incantations, potions and prayers of the traditional healer, whom Olson calls a witch doctor, had been unsuccessful. Olson offered her Terramycin as a possible cure, but she rejected it, saying, "You are white. Your ways are different from ours."[9]

Olson could have easily convinced some individuals to apply the Terramycin to their eyes, and when they got well the superiority of his ways over the traditional healer's would have been proved. But believing that this would establish a competitive and adversarial relationship that could destroy the healer's role in the culture and in effect destroy her by heaping shame on her powers, Olson looked for an alternative. Sensing that there was not a demonic element in her practice of traditional medicine, he waited for God's timing.

Five days later, having contracted pinkeye himself, he went to the traditional healer and asked her for help. She performed the routine but to no avail. Olson returned to her, showing that he had received no relief. He then asked her to perform her incantations again but this time to put the Terramycin in his eyes as well. Since she was already looking bad from having no positive effect on the pinkeye epidemic, she decided she had nothing to lose. In three days Olson's eyes, unlike everyone else's, were clear of the illness. Now the problem was how to get the cure to the others without offending the traditional healer.

I waited for the right time to talk to her again. I didn't want to insult her in any way. One evening I saw her walk out of the home, her shoulders stooped with fatigue. I followed her outside into the dark and caught her arm. She turned around.

I held up the tube of Terramycin. "Why don't you try this potion?" I said. "You cured my eyes with it. Perhaps it will work with your people as well."

Within three days she had cured everyone. It increased her stature in the home. She was proud of having been effective with her chants and her new potion, and became a good friend of mine—also a channel for other health measures.[10]

Eventually the traditional healer would introduce disinfectants into the tribal ceremonies, followed by other health measures and eventually health centers administered and staffed by Motilones. This became one of the great success stories in community development. From Olson's experience I have extracted several principles that can be used as guidelines:

1. Whenever possible, choose friendship over confrontation.

2. Use local ceremony, technology and personnel in the introduction of change as often as possible.

3. Introduce change in such a way that it does not violate the patterns and roles of people with vested interest and in a way which does not exalt yourself.

4. Build upon what is known and practiced (for example, vaccination was introduced as another form of traditional bloodletting).

5. Ensure that sustaining the change does not depend upon the presence of the outsider.

6. Keep central the role of the Holy Spirit, for "without Him, there would have been no real or lasting development."[11]

A situation that could easily have split the village and turned friends and family against each other was so wisely handled that in time all the villagers gave their lives to the living Christ and saw him as a Motilone who walked their trails.

I am particularly impressed by the way Olson did not need to be seen as the one providing the answers, the healing medicine, the one who deserved the credit. Even his approaching the witch doctor at night so she could be protected from any public shame reveals a profound humility, unlike the conspicuous "humility" many of us prefer.

Summary

Westerners, simply by being themselves, create conflict because they operate from a different value base. Directness, confrontation, forthrightness and candid outspokenness are valued and expected in Western culture (though politeness and respect should not be compromised when exercising these values). In most of the world these same values, even when demonstrated respectfully, are considered rude, unrefined, ill-mannered, discourteous and even contemptuous. It is easy to see how quickly misunderstanding, miscommunication and conflict emerge. Parties who intend openness and friendship toward each other instead come across as insensitive at best, arrogant at worst. Few events are more tragic than when two parties try to communicate friendship but are perceived by each other as communicating indifference and hostility. But a few relatively painless adjustments can change that.

PART 2

CULTURAL DIVERSITY AND CONFLICT RESOLUTION

5
MEDIATION
AND THE
MEDIATOR

In all fighting, the direct method may
be used for joining battle but indirect methods
will be needed to secure victory.
SUN TZU

Culture shock blasted the ears of Pat and Steve the very first night
they moved into their house in Jakarta, Indonesia.[1] As they were
getting their children ready for bed, talking and praying, there
was a sudden siren blast. It was the Muslim call to prayer.

Steve and Pat soon learned that the siren's source was very near their
house, with the speaker pointed in their direction. The siren went off
several times each day, and for them these blasts were not a major
problem. But the nightly disruption of their family time proved unbear-
ably frustrating. If the children were put to bed early, they would be
awakened by the noise of the siren screeching through their house.
Sometimes it frightened them.

With her patience wearing thin, Pat resolved to change the situation.
Back home in the United States a person with this sort of problem would
just go to the proper authorities, explain the problem and hope a solution

could be worked out. If not, one would appeal to higher authorities and to noise-abatement laws, if necessary.

As Pat prepared her speech to the authorities at the local mosque, a thought crossed her mind. Shortly before departing for Indonesia, she and her husband had attended a seminar on conflict resolution in the Two-Thirds World. The content started coming back to her, and quickly she realized that the approach she had envisioned would not work. In fact, it could do great damage. There was an alternative, and she began to think about how to make it happen. She would have to take an indirect approach.

Using a mediator was one of the seminar suggestions. But who? And how? Would it work? The whole idea seemed very awkward and unnatural. Yet it was worth a try. What was there to lose?

That evening, the guard Pat and Steve had hired to watch the house each night appeared for his usual 6:00 shift, and Pat realized that this person might be the answer she was seeking. He didn't have much status, and since she was new in Jakarta she had no idea of his network of relationships. Nevertheless, it was worth a try.

She explained the situation to the guard, and he in turn began to talk with other household guards in the area about Pat's dilemma. Eventually an area supervisor of these guards heard the story. The supervisor, as it happened, had a friend who worked at the mosque. The friend in the mosque talked with someone in authority.

This process of communication took a number of days. In the busyness of settling into her new home, Pat left behind her concern about the siren and almost forgot her conversation with the guard. But one night she realized that it had been some time since the mosque siren had disrupted the evening talks and prayers with her children. Had she simply become used to the sound and failed to notice it? Or had something changed?

The next night she listened carefully. The siren went off at the appointed time, but it was definitely quieter, and it seemed as though the loudspeaker was no longer pointed directly at their house.

"It works! Mediators really work!" was Pat's gleeful conclusion as she reported the story to me. Without realizing it, she had actually combined two indirect strategies for handling the conflict. The first, mediation, is the subject of this chapter; Pat's other strategy will be taken up in chapter six.

The Mediator

Using a mediator, a third person who acts as a middle person or intermediary between two opposing parties, is a common indirect strategy for handling conflict in the Two-Thirds World.[2] By definition a mediator avoids face-to-face confrontation, thereby minimizing the possibility of loss of face, shame or dishonor for both parties. David Augsburger elaborates:

> Western styles of conflict resolution value one-to-one direct address, confrontation, self-disclosure, negotiation, and resolution. . . . In the other two-thirds of the world, conflicts are immediately referred to a third party—an older, wiser, neutral, skilled family member or a trusted person from the community. Triangulation serves to save face for both parties and to reduce shaming in the system.[3]

The following story shows how a mediator can help resolve an interpersonal conflict.

Don and his wife, new missionaries in the Philippines, were progressing nicely in language and culture learning. They enjoyed the Filipinos. Their children, however, were having some difficulty. As they made their way to and from school, the Filipino children would tease them, call them names and sometimes throw things at them. The young Americans' dislike for the Filipino children soon approached hatred. They wanted to go home, go anywhere but the Philippines.

Don knew most of the parents of the offending Filipino children and entertained the idea of having a talk with them. He would be friendly, warm and very careful in handling the topic so as not to offend them.

But after pondering this approach, he discarded it. The risk was too great. A direct, face-to-face carefronting, even carefully done, would almost certainly cause them shame and loss of face. Any future ministry Don might have with those people would be jeopardized. How would the Filipinos handle a situation like this?

Don had been making friends with the merchants at the local market-place. Over the weeks he had observed that everyone related easily and with confidence to the butcher. In fact, in a rather uncanny way, this man seemed to be the broker of information for the entire community—an informal opinion leader. Don could build on this information to solve the problem.

One day, as Don approached, the butcher responded with a cheery "Hello, Mr. Collins. How are you today?"

Don replied, "I am not so well today."

"Oh, Mr. Collins, what is the problem?"

"We are feeling sadness," said Don.

"I'm so sorry, Mr. Collins. What causes you to be sad?"

"It is our children; they are very unhappy."

"Mr. Collins, that is very sad. What causes them to be unhappy?"

"Well, as they travel to school and back home they have some difficulties."

"What kind of difficulties, Mr. Collins?"

"It seems that sometimes rocks or sticks are thrown and unkind words are said to them. My wife and I love this country and the Filipino people so much. We are very sad that our children do not enjoy the Philippines as we do."

"I am so-o-o sorry, Mr. Collins. This is very bad. We are glad to have you in our country and want all of your family to be happy here. We must hope that your children will soon be happy too."

At this point Don bought some meat and, with a friendly farewell, moved on.

Within two or three days the problem was solved. His children were no longer being bothered, and in a short while their attitude began improving. What had happened?

After Don left the butcher, other shoppers had come by the butcher shop. After a greeting and "How are you?" from each shopper, the butcher would mention that he was sad today. The shopper would show sympathy and ask why. The butcher would say he had been talking to the new American in the community—"the long nose," a term often used for referring to Americans. The visitor would ask more questions until eventually the butcher unfolded the story.

Before long another community member would come into the shop, and the same scenario would transpire. As each visitor to the butcher shop made his or her way into other parts of the marketplace, the situation repeated itself. No fingers would be pointed, no names mentioned, no one would be directly confronted. Yet gradually everyone knew the problem, knew the "offenders" and knew what must be done.

Even though everyone knew which parents had children in the community and which children were likely to be responsible, no direct accusations were made; no one would by shamed by being held responsible for not showing proper courtesy and hospitality to the new guests. The community valued smooth and harmonious relationships, unity and peace among its members, and it had responsible ways of responding to disruptions. And while a few families may have been to blame, the entire community held itself accountable for maintaining its values, especially making the guests in their culture feel welcome.

Misinterpreted Overtures

Becoming aware that Don's children were feeling alienated, the community members began to find out why this was happening. It was not just the responsibility of the parents; everyone in the small community got involved, since what affected one member affected everyone. Everyone felt the burden of the problem and the burden of collective shame, so everyone shared in the effort to make things right. My Filipino friends tell me that the following is probably an accurate rendering of the events.

The Filipino parents and other community members probably began inquiring about the relationship between the local children and Don's children. They discovered that their own children were trying to make friends and believed that they were showing themselves friendly, but that the Americans refused to respond and instead drew inward. They seemed to resist the overtures of the Filipino children.

The parents and community members then asked what the young Filipinos did to show friendliness; the children responded that they tried to get their attention by tossing an occasional stick or stone. Hearing this, the parents realized that the American children would not interpret rock-throwing as friendship. They suggested alternative tactics to show their good intentions and develop friendships.

In Filipino culture, as in any culture, children have their ways of initiating relationships and showing the desire for friendship. Americans, of course, had no basis for interpreting the sticks and stones as friendship. But if we think about it in terms of how grade-school boys often express their interest in girls, it may be similar. The boy, in his awkwardness and bashfulness, will playfully throw paper at the girl, pull her hair or perform some other "unsocial" activity to get her attention and, he vaguely hopes, her friendship. It seems the same kind of thing was operating with the Filipino children.

Don's handling of the situation showed astute cultural insight. Doing the culturally appropriate thing in this delicate situation won him the respect of the people and therefore gained him credibility as a person and as a Christian. It is easier to listen to someone you respect, and Don had a message he hoped would be heard.

Analysis

Matsumoto provides an interesting analysis of this orientation toward group harmony from the Japanese perspective, but his insights have broader application. "In the West the relationship between Self and

Other is understood on the basis of confrontation,"[4] whereas in Japan "relationships are not based in power confrontations, but on harmony and balance."[5] He states that the strong dichotomizing between self and other in the Western worldview allows for interpersonal confrontations. No such sharp distinction exists in more holistic cultures, where definitions of "self" and "other" are blurred, reflecting mutuality, interdependence and contextual flexibility in a complex matrix of relationships.[6]

Note that even through a mediator it would still be very easy for Westerners to make direct accusations. Such an approach may seem culturally appropriate, but actually it would only aggravate the situation, for then the accused loses face not only before the accuser but also before the mediator and anyone else who may find out. Shame is compounded. It would be bad enough to be shamed by the guest in the community, but to be shamed before the esteemed mediator would be unbearable. As a general rule, blame should not be placed on another, not even through a mediator.

Exceptions to this principle do exist, however. Imagine two people in conflict with each other, with a third party, a mediator, standing between them. One party articulates a very direct complaint about the other person but speaks and looks only at the mediator. It is almost as if the opposing person is not present, yet he or she has heard and seen everything.

The mediator now turns to the other party and begins to repeat the accusations, but more objectively and with less passion. The other party now has her or his turn to respond while the mediator (and the accuser) listen. The mediator again repeats the story but attempts to clarify it and reduce the emotional pitch. Little by little, a resolution is reached.

This process seems a bit comical, even foolish, to the Westerner, but it works rather effectively in certain cultural contexts. It is an effective strategy for several reasons. First, the party speaking to the mediator is not directly putting down the other person, even though an onlooker may think so. The accusation is still indirect. Second, the mediator usually will not repeat each person's identical words, since the opposing party has been there and heard everything. The mediator sifts the words and accusations and tries to get at the core of the matter. Thus the mediator interprets and rephrases the words so they will be heard more accurately. Third, most conflicts have an emotional component. One party may be shouting his or her side of the story to the mediator, but the mediator, not caught up in the emotion of the matter, speaks more quietly and objectively, thus bringing an element of calm. While appearing awkward to the Westerner, this strategy has brought reconciliation and restored peace in many conflicts.

The Unwitting Mediator

Businesspeople, missionaries and most other Western expatriates, because they have perceived status and power, are often called upon to play the mediator role without realizing it. Someone comes to them with a problem that has arisen between her- or himself and another person. The Westerner, believing that sensitive face-to-face confrontation is the best way to handle conflict, tells the individual to go and talk it out with the other person. The Western Christian easily and confidently adds, "This is the biblical thing to do."

Two-Thirds-World people tend to find such a course of action quite unnatural, if not repulsive. They possess neither skill nor experience in direct confrontation. Furthermore, they wonder why the Westerners refuse to help. They have power and influence. The situation could be handled rather painlessly if they would only be willing to mediate. The indigenous people are confused, hurt and may lose confidence in the Westerners, who have the power but appear unwilling to solve the problem.

The Westerner, on the other hand, finds the indigenous person rather irresponsible in not wanting to face up to the problem. Words like "immature," "adolescent," "lacking in leadership" and "timid" may be applied to the person refusing to confront. With these thoughts lodged in the Westerner's mind, a distrust sets in, placing a strain on the relationship.

Massive miscommunication is taking place. Both parties are doing exactly what is appropriate in their respective cultures. But when each comes to the relationship with only one set of lenses to interpret a given situation, the result is misunderstanding and a weakening of the relationship. The motives of both are innocent, but the consequences are serious.

The Purpose of a Mediator

While most mediators become involved to resolve conflict, some have other purposes. For example, a mediator may be used to *cause* conflict. Throughout Africa and parts of Asia, particularly India, witch doctors, priests, sorcerers and other kinds of mediums are available to cast spells, perform incantations, practice exorcisms and communicate with the dead. While the mediator performs many of these activities in order to acquire some favor for the seeker (such as getting over an illness, obtaining a job, being healed of infertility), many times the mediator is called on to bring ill upon the seeker's enemy. The mediator may cast a spell, pronounce a curse or require the seeker to do something that will bring negative consequences upon the enemy. Such activity is intended to settle a grievance. It is an indirect way of getting even, settling the score, seeking justice.

People who are called on to act as mediators usually possess some power, influence, status, prestige or authority. They operate at different levels in society, and depending upon one's own status, and to some extent one's relationships, one mediator will be chosen over another. It is always preferable to choose a mediator who understands your own perspective and holds considerable influence with the other party. Yet if the mediator is perceived as too partial to be objective, he or she will be discounted by the other party.

Matsumoto explains the purpose of a mediator: "The need for a

mediator is a sign that unity is the ideal in relationship."[7] There is more
to this rather basic platitude than is first obvious. In the Two-Thirds
World, conflict is a violation of community solidarity and peace, not just
a breach between two people. Bringing shame on another is not an
individual act but necessarily affects immediate and extended family,
friends and associates.

This intense interdependence and group orientation confuses the
Westerner, who thinks of the individual as a free, independent, self-
determining person. But the group spirit has been firmly entrenched
throughout much of the world—probably because group survival depended on it. In solidarity people can stand against an army; in solidarity
people can survive natural disaster by sharing resources; in solidarity
people have a stable history and identity; in solidarity people enjoy
protection and security; in solidarity people celebrate many friendships.
Solidarity has numerous benefits, and the mediator serves as their
guardian.

The Ultimate Punishment and Shame
Romanucci-Ross, commenting from her research in a Mexican village,
offers yet another perspective. Although group solidarity must not be
jeopardized, it is really the offender's place in the group that is in
jeopardy. Persistent or gross violations of solidarity will result in the
offender's becoming "que no es de aquí—an outsider and nonentity, 'not
of here' or of anywhere else either."[8] One's membership in the group
and one's individual identity are inseparable. To be cast out of a group
is to be stripped of identity, even personhood. Continual shaming of
others calls forth the ultimate punishment—the shame of being an
outcast, no longer a member of a group, outside of solidarity, unpro-
tected, vulnerable and exposed, living in a perpetual state of shame and
nonidentity.

Perhaps this is part of what Matthew (18:17) and Paul (1 Cor 5:11-13)
had in mind:

If he refuses to listen to them, tell it to the church; and if he refuses to listen even to the church, treat him as you would a pagan or tax collector [an outsider, outcast, nonperson].

But now I am writing you that you must not associate with anyone who calls himself a brother but is sexually immoral or greedy, an idolater or a slanderer, a drunkard or a swindler. With such a man do not even eat.

What business is it of mine to judge those outside the church? Are you not to judge those inside? God will judge those outside. "Expel the wicked man from among you."

The person who habitually continues in sin with seemingly little or no effort to change, yet still wants to be known as a Christian, should not be treated as one who is in solidarity with the church. That seems to be the thrust of the two statements.

The Mediator's Intentions

Matsumoto expands on the ultimate intention of the mediator. Mediation takes place, obviously, between two people or two parties. The intended outcome is not simply for mutual tolerance, physical coexistence or a superficial feeling good about each other. It goes deeper. "Self and Other are completed in the relationship. Both have a feeling of identity and certainty, through the work of the mediator."[9]

The mediator serves not simply to reconcile, interpret and negotiate but, much more positively, to *integrate* two parties. The mediatorial role is not to strive for a plurality of individuals but for a "strong consciousness of belonging to the same group"[10] that can be characterized as a bonding of the hearts, minds and souls, a bonding in which identities mingle and unite. Thus personhood is discovered and affirmed in community.

Only in such a context does being a pagan or outcast become the ultimate shame and punishment. Solidarity of this nature is a concept hardly understood in Western cultures and rarely experienced. Yet the Bible employs extensive language to highlight similar values: "body," "church," "unity," "oneness" and "fellowship." One thing is certain: conflict-resolution skills are important for the church everywhere.

Characteristics of a Mediator

Foremost, the mediator needs to be seen as a respected, neutral, objective third party who is capable of weighing out fairness in the resolution of a conflict. The mediator must be trusted by both parties to come up with a solution that will protect them from shame. While the central issue is justice, the outcome needs to be win-win, no losers. There are some exceptions to this, but generally it holds true. The abilities to listen impartially, suspend judgment and accurately gather and assess information are other important characteristics. Finally, to function effectively the mediator must have power (financial, status, position), so that both parties will take seriously and abide by the mediator's judgment. If one party refuses to cooperate, he or she should fear the possibility of being shamed and losing face before the mediator and the whole community. If that real possibility does not enter the minds of both parties, the mediator will be ineffective.

In several countries mediators are still used to find a bride for a man. Usually this is a job for the parents, and they in turn employ the services of a mediator. Because this event takes much planning, the parents will try to identify the mediator well in advance. Since these services sometimes require remuneration, money must be saved. Or in some cases parents try to do a number of favors for the mediator so that he or she will feel indebtedness and perform the service as a kind of repayment.

The parents will try to get the most influential mediator possible, to boost their chances of being approved by the potential bride's parents. The young woman's parents will not want to risk shame by turning down a request from such an important person—so the reasoning goes. Of course, the higher-ranked the mediator, the higher the cost of the services.

Everyone experiences a certain amount of stress in the process. The parents of the potential groom wonder how much money it will take and who is the best person for that money. Should they spend more or even borrow money in their effort to secure the best mediator and the best bride? The young woman's parents experience stress since they want their daughter to marry the best person available, which usually means the person with the most education, status or wealth. (In these situations love is generally a nonissue until after the marriage.) If the young woman's parents turn down the mediator who represents the would-be groom and his parents, will a better prospect come along? The mediator must be successful most of the time or will lose the status of a good mediator.

Complicating the process is the fact that turning down the mediator is also a snub of the potential groom and his parents. The snub, real or perceived will likely generate conflict between the families. If the parties are not careful, the entire community can take sides. One way to alleviate this eventuality is for the young woman's family to identify a flaw that would make her a less desirable prospect. They might say, "She is sickly," or "She may not be able to bear children," or "She will make a poor mother and worker." Although none of these statements may be true, and probably everyone knows they aren't, they do provide a way for the young man's parents to withdraw their request for a perfectly legitimate reason. Everyone saves face, at least at the surface, and peace is preserved.

Biblical Principles

Did God ever face conflict? How did he handle it? God was, in fact, involved in the greatest conflict in history, a conflict that was cosmic in scope. The conflict, caused by humanity's sin, resulted in a broken relationship between creature and Creator. Here began a global conflict of a proportion unique in history. How should God handle it? Face to face? Direct confrontation? Carefronting? Avoiding? We can be eternally grateful that God chose none of these.

The enmity between God and humans could be healed and unity restored only through a mediator—an indirect method. Only one person was qualified to mediate this cosmic conflict, Jesus Christ (Jn 3:17; Heb 7—8).

> For there is one God and one mediator between God and men, the man Christ Jesus, who gave himself as a ransom for all men. (1 Tim 2:5-6)

Kenneth Wuest defines *mediator* in this verse as "one who intervenes between two, either in order to make or restore peace and friendship or to form a compact or ratify a covenant."[11] Wuest continues: "Our Lord is a mediator in that He interposed Himself by His death, and made possible the restoration of the harmony between God and man which had been broken by sin. The distinctive word for 'man' here is not *aner,* 'a male individual,' but *anthropos,* the . . . generic term."[12]

William Hendriksen states that "Christ is the One who has voluntarily taken his stand between the offended God and the offending sinner, in order to take upon himself the wrath of God which the sinner has deserved, thereby delivering the latter."[13]

Consider Romans 5:10-11: "For if, when we were God's enemies, we were reconciled to him through the death of his Son, how much more, having been reconciled, shall we be saved through his life! Not only is this so, but we also rejoice in God through our Lord Jesus Christ, through whom we have now received reconciliation." From this passage Hendriksen draws great encouragement for us all:

> We will not be disappointed in our hope, for, in Christ, God loves us so deeply that the Savior *died* for us while we were still sinners. If, then, we were justified by that *death*—or that blood—of Christ, much more shall we be saved from any future outpouring of God's wrath.[14]
>
> If God justifies and reconciles to himself enemies, he will *certainly* save friends.[15]

Mediators are frequently referred to in other Scriptures. The apostle Paul notes that Moses was a mediator in delivering the Law (Gal 3:19-20; cf.

Ex 32:30-32; Num 12:6-8). Job, in his response to Bildad, longs for a mediator who could arbitrate (Job 9:33). An alienated father and son, David and Absalom, were reconciled (temporarily) through the mediation of Joab (2 Sam 14:1-23). It is reasonable to see the prophets' role in mediatorial terms: they were standing between humans and God (Deut 18:18-23). Then, of course, there is the intermediary function of the Old Testament priest, who bridged the God-human relationship (Ex 28:1; Lev 9:7; 16:6; cf. Heb 5:1-4).

Summary

Because of a concern for maintaining community and family solidarity, many cultures of the world prefer indirect methods for handling conflict and potential conflict. One of the more common indirect methods is the use of a mediator. Neither the existence of a mediator nor the functions of a mediator are foreign to the scriptural account. While society may have contaminated the role of mediator or used it for selfish, even evil purposes, it is still a legitimate role that needs to be understood and appropriately employed by Christians.

6
THE ONE-DOWN POSITION AND VULNERABILITY

These eggs want salt [this person wants more than he is saying].
NICARAGUAN PROVERB

Many situations do not lend themselves to the use of a mediator for several reasons: lack of time, availability of the right person to mediate or nature of the conflict. Putting oneself in the one-down posture may be another culturally appropriate alternative when one is confronted with a situation of real or potential conflict.

Taking the one-down position means you make yourself vulnerable to another person or indicate that without their help you are in danger of being shamed or losing face. You put yourself in debt, obligation or obvious deference to the other party. By taking the position of need and calling on another for assistance, you utilize another twist on the notion of shame or loss of face.

Here is the way it works. It is important for you not to cause another person to lose face or be shamed, but if there is danger of this happening to *you,* you may call on another to protect you from losing face. In fact, you may even call on the very one who is endangering your honor to save you from the shame that may befall you. Generally, if one holds the power to keep another person from being shamed, that person is morally obligated to do something to keep shame from coming to the other. However, if the person does not act to save another's honor, she or he is in danger of losing face and being shamed. The next story illustrates how it works.

The Restaurant Manager

My friend "Mr. Collins" organized a party for his missionary colleagues at a local Filipino restaurant. The event was a farewell gathering for a family leaving for furlough. Mr. Collins and the restaurant manager had orally agreed on a total package price for the meal.

After a delightful feast, the waiter brought Don the bill, which turned out to be considerably more than had been agreed upon. Don had a conflict.

The direct method—some form of gracious confrontation to determine whether this was an honest mistake or an attempted fraud— seemed to be the best and most efficient way of handling the situation. But honest mistake or not, this approach would cause shame and loss of face, because the implication would be obvious: the manager had failed. Furthermore, the failure would cause Don to lose face before his friends. Whether it was intentional or not was secondary. Don valued his relationship with the manager and did not want to risk losing it.

Some would argue that Don should have had the agreement in writing. But requiring a written contract would have communicated distrust early in the relationship. Don had resisted, hoping to stay consistent with local cultural patterns as much as possible.

Don could have simply given in and paid the bill, no questions asked. He could have borrowed from his friends to cover the cost; at least this would have avoided confrontation. However, if he had given in, the manager would have lost respect for Don, seeing him as weak and easy to manipulate.

An indirect approach held the only hope for achieving Don's most valued goal: maintaining the relationship in an atmosphere of honesty and mutual respect. So Don asked to see the manager.

After a friendly exchange of greetings, the inevitable question came from the manager: "Have you enjoyed the evening?"

Don explained that all had enjoyed themselves greatly; the food was very good, and the event was a success. Then, almost parenthetically, he added that there was one slight difficulty and he was feeling quite embarrassed.

The manager asked about the cause of his embarrassment, and Don responded, "I am so embarrassed and ashamed because I thought the price for the evening was going to be [a certain amount]. Now I find out it is much more expensive than I thought. I collected this amount from all of my friends, who came thinking that would be sufficient to cover the bill. The bill is much more than I expected. I do not have the money to pay the extra amount myself, and it will be very humiliating to ask my friends to pay more than I told them they would have to pay. They have enjoyed the evening so much here in your restaurant. I will be so ashamed if I have to ask them for more money."

The manager sympathized with Don's dilemma and took the bill back to his office. In a few moments he returned and said, "Will this help you, Mr. Collins?" The new total was considerably less, within a few dollars of the original amount agreed upon. Don decided the small amount left to pay was not worth quibbling about, and he thanked the manager profusely. Both walked away happy, with honor and respect intact.

Don had been careful not to make any accusations. The manager probably knew he had overcharged, and he knew that Don was aware. Yet to point a finger, accuse or try to place fault would have strained the relationship for a long while and perhaps destroyed any future opportunities for Don to establish a Christian witness.

Would you have paid the extra few dollars? Why or why not? Why do you think the manager did not come back with the originally agreed-upon price? How would you have responded to the much higher bill? To the few dollars over the original price? Real everyday situations like this require an understanding of cultural values, how those values are expressed and what the appropriate responses are. Simply doing what you do back in your home culture will not work. Different cultures play by different rules. Unless those rules blatantly violate Scripture, you should seriously consider understanding them and abiding by them.

Don was in danger of being shamed before his friends. By putting himself in the one-down position—that is, in jeopardy of being shamed and in need of protection—he gave the restaurant manager the power to save Don's face, protecting him from shame. While it is a violation of cultural standards to bring shame on another, it is a greater shame to be able to protect someone from shame and deliberately refuse to do it—that is, to intentionally expose their shame.

One more loose end: why did the manager come back with a figure a few dollars over the original amount? If he had come back with the exact amount agreed upon, he would have lost face by exposing the fact that he had violated the agreement intentionally. He did not shame himself in this way. At the same time, he was not willing to offer a lower price and lose money. Don wisely did not push the issue. He valued the relationship more than a few dollars. Besides, he realized that the manager would probably not try this again, now it was clear that Don knew how to navigate in Filipino culture and would not easily be manipulated.

Some might argue that such a conflict resolution style can itself be manipulative. Yes, it can be, but properly understood it can be positive. We all respect people who wisely apply cultural tools to sustain important cultural values. In the Philippines the one-down position is a tool to achieve justice without violating other important values. The person who uses this tool wisely is respected and held in esteem; he or she has credibility. But Filipinos can usually tell when someone is using the same cultural tools to manipulate. That person will lose credibility, and so will his or her message.

Intentional Public Shaming

Intentionally exposing another's shame does happen, but only when one party chooses to publicly declare an antagonistic or adversarial relationship with another. On such occasions indirectness is abandoned and directness takes over in an attempt to heap shame on the other person and widely discredit her or him. People who have guest status, like Don, rarely suffer such public humiliation.

Public humiliation is carried out at the national level as well. During the Korean Olympic games, a Korean boxer lost a match with an American. The Korean's manager became so distraught that he lost control, climbed into the ring, jumped on the back of the American boxer and began to pound his fists on him. We are left to wonder what prompted such an unusual response. Did the manager feel great shame at losing? Was his job at stake? We can only surmise.

But any concern for the manager was quickly forgotten when American television networks broadcast the unfortunate incident throughout the world. It was bad enough that Korea should be embarrassed by the conduct of the manager, but now to have that shame played over and over again before the world was a national humiliation. The Korean government became very upset at the multiple replaying of that disgraceful moment. The manager had committed a shameful act, but for those who had represented themselves as friends to compound that shame by repeatedly displaying it to the world was hard to understand and even harder to forgive.

When a nation feels it has been shamed before the world, it will feel quite free to humiliate representatives from the shaming nation. In part this explains the actions of Iranians and, more recently, Iraqis toward United States citizens in their countries or toward the United States as a nation. Angry demonstrations, name-calling, burning flags and figures in effigy and other symbols of shaming can be seen as attempts to restore national face and national honor. Westerners find this very difficult to understand.

The Siren Revisited

In the last chapter I told how Pat and Steve used a mediator to deal with the problem of the local mosque's loud siren calling people to prayer. The siren went off each evening just as Pat and Steve were enjoying family time and putting the children to bed. Pat found that their night guard served as a good mediator who took his responsibility seriously and brought a happy conclusion to the matter.

Pat's communication with the guard is worth noting since it beautifully illustrates the one-down posture for trying to manage conflict. When she talked with the guard, she did not blame, accuse or show anger or frustration. She did describe their family times and how important it was to them to talk quietly with their children, put them to bed and then have a peaceful night. But sometimes, she said, they could hardly hear each other because the siren was rather loud. When the children went to bed early, they would be awakened by the noise—in their home country there were no sirens. Sometimes they became frightened and said they did not want to stay in this country. Pat told the guard how sad this made her feel, since they all wanted to be happy in Indonesia.

Pat handled a delicate situation very wisely. Suppose she had decided to use a mediator but was far less tactful, perhaps expressing considerable frustration and openly blaming the mosque authorities. One of two things might have transpired. If Pat had already won the night guard's respect, he would still have acted as a mediator, but in speaking to the other guards he probably would have reinterpreted her remarks to make them culturally appropriate. In other words, he would have protected her "face" so she would not lose respect.

If she had not won the guard's respect, on the other hand, he would have passed on the story as she told it, knowing full well that his friends' respect for her would diminish and they would put forth little effort on her behalf. But even more would be happening beneath the surface. The word would get out: these Americans are insensitive to cultural realities. Esteem for Steve and Pat would diminish. Their ministry efforts would be hindered; over time they might see few results; then they might blame the "hardness of the people" when they should have been examining themselves.

Fortunately, Pat handled the problem wisely, respect for her and her husband increased, and they are on their way to an effective ministry.

The Japanese, Television and Conflict

Another illustration: A Japanese businessman was putting up a large building in the midst of small private homes in Japan. An American friend noticed that all the TV wires from the surrounding houses had been attached to the uncompleted steel structure. He gives the following account.

Were he [the Japanese businessman] an American colleague or friend I might have said, "You aren't going to leave that mess of wires like that after the building is done, are you?" But such an implied criticism and the bold imputing of ugliness would have been totally wrong with a Japanese friend. So I tried a positive approach, complete with an implied compliment. . . . "Your neighbors are likely very happy to have such a nice high place to put their TV antenna." . . .

He [the Japanese businessman] began to tell the whole story. . . . Now he was telling it on his own terms and in a context of acceptance rather than criticism. . . . It turned out that while the first major structural steel was being erected for the frame of the building, the households of the nearby cluster began having trouble with their TV reception. The higher the steel, the worse it got. . . .

Neither the construction crew nor my friend, the owner, was aware of the problem. It would be rare for any individual to come to complain about such a thing. Such boldness is bad manners among the Japanese. Instead, these householders talked to each other and came to a very Japanese conclusion about what should be done. One of the older men in the neighborhood was selected as a messenger to approach the owner on behalf of all the households. An old person is presumed to be wise and deserving of great respect; any message such a person carries must be given attention as a matter of honor. He was not sent empty-handed. The people of the neighborhood had each contributed money so that an expensive gift could be purchased to serve as one of the key elements in this age-old ritual of the aggrieved.

After all was in readiness, the old man visited my friend in his home, presented the gift, and assured him of the best wishes of all of the householders. And, oh yes, by the way, was he aware that there was this one little problem? Of course, it was surely not more than a simple coincidence, and the people were certain that he had nothing to do with it, but the television signal from the city was now almost gone. Did he have any idea what these poor householders might do so that they could have television again?[1]

A study showed that the building was causing the problem, and at considerable expense to the contractor, action was taken to correct the problem to everyone's satisfaction. "What made him do it?" asks Ted Ward, who was the American in this story. Not fear of litigation, community protests or boycotts but "honor."[2]

By using the one-down position, one says, "We are having a problem"—or, more literally, "A problem has come upon us"—(passive voice), rather than "Your building is blocking the TV signal" (active voice). The indirect method indicates a need without assigning blame and suggests that perhaps someone could help. The direct method says you are to blame, we are holding you accountable and you better do something about it or risk a lawsuit.

Teaching in China

Being allowed to stay in a country, getting a visa renewed or just getting cooperation from superiors may depend on culturally wise handling of sensitive issues and sensitive people. A young Western woman teaching English in China found the one-down position strategic in dealing with government officials, a category of people very sensitive to shame and loss of face.

Chinese officials paid a visit to Joani in her classroom. Very graciously they requested that she increase her teaching load from sixteen to twenty hours a week. To a typical North American, any of several responses would seem natural and acceptable:

☐ "I am sorry, but my contract calls for sixteen hours, and I think it best to stay with that."

☐ "Let me call my supervisor, and he/she can discuss it with you."

☐ "I would really like to help you out, but my schedule is full right now. Maybe next term."

These options, though understood in Western culture, would have produced embarrassment and loss of face for the Chinese officials. Joani handled it differently: "This is something I would really like to do. But I have a fear. I fear that if I teach twenty hours a week I will not be able to do such a good job for you and the students." Interpreted, this means that she would risk shame and loss of face before her students and her supervisors if she had to teach an extra four hours a week. The extra four hours would make her less effective.

If the Chinese officials forced her to do it, they would be putting her at risk of losing face. By putting herself in the one-down position, in jeopardy of losing face, she shifted the onus back on the officials to shelter her from this unfortunate eventuality. The officials understood and withdrew their request.[3]

Dealing with Authorities

Westerners in the Two-Thirds World soon discover that dealing with authorities is one of their most sensitive challenges. Getting papers signed, getting permissions granted and negotiating border transitions can be most precarious enterprises and severe tests of patience. Direct approaches such as demanding, raising the voice, implied threats and other "muscle" tactics usually only delay the results and can work against the Westerner. The one-down indirect strategy, however, serves one well in these situations.

A relatively new community-development worker had her mother visiting in the country.[4] Foreigners need to be registered and often require documents if they are to travel freely in the country. When she tried to secure the necessary documents, the new worker was told that her mother's return air ticket had to be produced before the internal travel documents could be issued. They didn't have the ticket with them; it was at the house. They talked with the authorities about options. It appeared there were none. The gray-haired mother soon became weary and found a seat.

The worker then began a different approach. "I feel so terrible. I foolishly forgot to bring the ticket. It is entirely my fault that we are having this problem. I am so ashamed, because I desperately wanted to impress my mother with my ability to take care of her once she arrived in the country. This is so humiliating. What must my mother be thinking?"

And she had yet another problem. If she took her mother on the long drive home to get the ticket and then returned with her to sign the documents, her mother would be too tired, and her health was fragile. If she left her mother at the office while she went home, her husband would be upset that she had driven home alone in the darkness. Besides, her mother would be very uncomfortable if she had to stay alone and might become fearful. It was a distressing situation, and she was so very sorry for causing the authorities these problems. Was there anything that could be done?

The authorities, sensing how important it was to protect her from being shamed before her own mother, decided to believe that her mother indeed had a return air ticket. They officially stamped the papers; the two women thanked the authorities profusely for their extraordinary kindness and were soon on their way without further complication.

Bribes and Conflict

Those who travel abroad are aware that bribes are often extorted in situations like the one I've just described. While this is a reality of travel in the Two-Thirds World, it is not an easy situation for the Westerner to understand or handle. Many times government officials and civil servants are paid minimum wage or less, since their superiors know that bribes will supplement their salary and allow them to earn a livable income. Most Western organizations have a formal "no bribes" policy. But what are the alternatives? There is a "rule of thumb" strategy that usually works and will rarely do harm.

First, approach the officials (government, corporate, religious, police, community) with obvious courtesy and deference. Use the appropriate greetings and opening formalities common to the culture. At the appropriate time, make your request or concern known, but with gentleness and meekness. Any sign of impatience or frustration will work against you.

Second, assuming step one did not get you to your goal, use the one-down position, describing the humiliation and shame that awaits you if you are unable to get these documents (or whatever your need is). It is wise to apologize to the authorities for causing them to use their valuable time and energy listening to your problem. Also, if you have been negligent at any point or have overlooked a requirement, no matter how foolish and pointless it may seem to you, apologize for that. Ask if there is any way they can think of that you might be helped. Do not demand!

Third, assuming you are still unsuccessful, wait—and wait some more. Sooner or later the authorities will realize that a bribe is not forthcoming and they will be better off getting rid of you. Your hanging around indefinitely will prove an embarrassment to them, because the message to others is that they cannot help you; and that is to their shame, since they are the authorities.

On one occasion I was told there was no way I could get a document. It was important that I secure it, so I decided to ask questions—any question I could think of that related to my problem—and probe for any opening that I could use. The line behind me was getting longer, but I knew if I stepped aside I would lose my chance. So I gently persisted. The woman at the desk was very patient with me and seemingly could not tell me to move on. Finally, with the long line shuffling restlessly, and for reasons known only to her, she gave me the document.

My friend had a similar problem, but the officials flatly told him to step aside and come back tomorrow. He had been given this line several days in a row, though, and this time he was prepared. He said, "I will wait over here on the side until the proper authority comes along who can handle my request." With that he sat down on the floor, pulled out some reading material and began to snack on sandwiches.

People began to stare and asked the authorities why the American was sitting on the floor like this. The embarrassment of not being able to help a guest in their culture prompted the authorities to grant him the documents he needed within the hour.

This kind of persistence is a more extreme strategy. Use it only when the help you are seeking is essential and there is no other alternative for getting it.

And though you have not paid a bribe, I strongly recommend that within forty-eight hours after obtaining your request you return to that official expressing gratitude and possibly with a gift that would be fitting to his or her status and service to you. A cake for the family (or the office workers), a toy for the children, a pen or some similar gift would show appreciation for the courtesy extended to you.

Remember that you, a Westerner, almost certainly have more money than the Two-Thirds people you are dealing with. It is important to show kindness and generosity in appropriate ways other than bribes. Otherwise, you and other Westerners may legitimately be perceived as selfish and ungrateful.

Variations on the One-Down Position
The stories I've told illustrate the basic concept of the one-down ap-

proach to handling conflict. Variations exist which complicate matters but which must be understood if we are to choose the best option in a given situation.

Social status and shame. It appears there are degrees in the shaming process that can obscure the issues. These degrees are related to position and social status, which are often more important in Two-Thirds World cultures than in Western culture. A lower-status person is automatically in a one-down position, having less power and being more vulnerable. Many societies have an elaborate pecking order from the most powerful to the most powerless. The nature and degree of shame depend on where people are in the social order.

For example, causing someone (or allowing someone) beneath you in status to be shamed is not as serious as causing someone above you to be shamed. A person of higher status may cause or allow people in a lower status to experience shame (1) to "keep them in their place," (2) to enhance the higher-status person's authority or (3) to signal to the lower-status people that there is no future in this relationship, so they should start looking elsewhere for help.

The Christian finds such practices discriminatory and unbiblical. Such concern with status needs to be challenged with the clear teaching of Scripture. Yet not all situations are so clear, and there is the major problem of how to confront. For these reasons some social situations create a conflict for Christians. Often higher- and lower-status people attend the same social functions. The higher-status people cluster together and generally are at the center of activity. Lower-status people, at the periphery, also cluster, but the two groups have limited or no interchange. More specifically, the higher-status people resist association with those in lower status. In some cultures, any hint of egalitarianism seems to be a repulsive concept. So what is the Christian to do?

Westerners in Two-Thirds World countries often find themselves assigned to a high status because of their comparative wealth, education and influence. What is the best way for a Christian to deal with this position?

Some Christians determine in advance to focus their ministry efforts on high-status people. Such a focus means they need to consider what kind of automobile(s) to buy, what kind of house to live in, what kind of tableware to use, what kind of clothes to wear and so on. To fulfill cultural expectations, they will need to mingle socially with high-status people at public events. In this way they can build trust and gradually take on the role necessary for becoming part of the "in-group." But they must be cautious not to form a partnership that is unbiblical, even though it may be culturally expedient.

Now suppose Western Christians deliberately participate in a social event with a lower-status group. Although this may be a biblically prophetic statement, it might be unwise in the long term. It would surely break trust with the higher-status group, members of which may be responsible for renewing visas or granting permission to work in a given region.

Some argue that too much association with lower-status people would probably make them feel uncomfortable anyway, since they would find such behavior from Westerners quite abnormal and awkward. While I find this argument without foundation, it might be part of the larger picture. The problem, then, is how to maintain trust with different status groups while preserving a biblical impartiality (Jas 2:1-9).

A solution that protects the prophetic element (confronting a cultural practice that violates Scripture) yet preserves trust with both groups is to spend the majority of the evening with your own status group but to periodically and briefly move over to the other group, greeting those you know, extending courtesies and even meeting new people. In this way you might be a curiosity but will not break trust. Furthermore, you will be honoring those who did not expect it, the lower-status group, without violating protocol. Honor is offered to both groups. Trust and relationship are sustained with both.

You might argue that this is just a more subtle form of discrimination. Perhaps that is true. If so, you must take a stand against the very idea of status—and there you certainly risk complete alienation from those in higher status.

Should we accommodate to the effects of sin in this world? If so, how? If not, at what price? How much should we take local cultural values into consideration? These are tough questions, and easy answers elude the one who tries to be both culturally sensitive and biblically true.

In-group, out-group and shame. Another variation on the one-down position relates to the category one is perceived to occupy in a culture. It is not related to status so much as to what one might call the "inner circle." Bringing shame on someone in the "out-group" is not nearly so serious as shaming someone in the "in-group." In-group persons have strong bonds of commitment to protect each other from shame. While one does not usually shame anyone deliberately, it is a less serious violation if the person shamed is from the out-group.

As North Americans, both Joani and Don (whose stories were told earlier) were in a special category—the category of "guest." As they discovered, the people of their host country felt bound to do everything possible not to bring shame on a guest. In this sense a guest is parallel to a member of the in-group.

One-down, gift-giving and shame. Gift-giving, normally an innocent expression of thoughtfulness, can be turned into a form of dehumanizing indebtedness whereby those who receive eventually find themselves under heavy obligation to the one who gives. This is a way of putting and keeping people in a one-down position so they can be controlled. As people are put in debt through the receiving of gifts and favors, they soon are beholden to fulfill any request of the donor or risk being shamed. Giving gifts can be a shrewd if not vicious form of gaining power over others, keeping them in the one-down position so the donor can continually extract favors that further his or her own power.

After Abram heroically rescued many of the king of Sodom's subjects and much of his wealth, which had been taken by enemies, the king generously said to Abram, "Give me the people and keep the goods for yourself." Abram gave a response that is somewhat surprising: "I have raised my hand to the LORD, God Most High, Creator of heaven and earth, and have taken an oath that I will accept nothing belonging to you, not even a thread or the thong of a sandal, so that you will never be able to say, 'I made Abram rich' "(Gen 14:17-23). Was this response motivated by Abram's sense that he would be in great obligation to the king if he accepted all this wealth?

If one chooses to take the one-down position to solve a conflict, it is a viable cultural form. If, however, one is forced into a one-down position by the power or wealth of another, it becomes an unbiblical use of power and brings shame, loss of face. Everyone working in Two-Thirds World culture must be alert to this possibility. A generous person may, in fact, create a sense of indebtedness within the beneficiaries, such that they are robbed of their dignity and find themselves in a role of servitude. Eventually this awareness turns bitter and surfaces as anger, resentment and other forms of rebellion.

In order to avert this unfortunate byproduct of generosity, it is wise to channel generosity anonymously through a third party such as a local church, a not-for-profit agency or some highly trusted person who can act as a mediator of your kindness. Exercising this kind of caution protects everyone and offers several advantages:

☐ it does not create dependency or indebtedness toward the donor;

☐ the donor does not need to worry about a pseudofriendship from the receiver;

☐ it decreases the potential for power abuse in the relationship;

☐ it increases the likelihood that God rather than the donor will get the glory;

☐ it protects the dignity and self-esteem of the receiver;

☐ it helps maintain open and honest communication in the relationship, which is usually sacrificed when one is forced or pressured into a one-down position;

☐ it allows for a relationship of equals wherein each is free to mediate Christ to the other.

Public and private shame. To be shamed in public, especially before one's family, friends or fellow in-group members, is the most devastating form of shaming. Shame, by Two-Thirds World definition, is humiliation before important people. One experiences less shame if it comes at the private level or in situations where the shamed person is unknown to others.

Thus if one experiences a problem (or sin) with another person from a shame culture, it is wise to follow the apostle Matthew's advice and "show him his fault, just between the two of you" (Mt 18:15). Only in cases of ongoing resistance to deal with the problem or sin does one introduce the possibility of public shame.

Biblical Guidelines

Because it is risky to infer intentionality, we cannot be sure where the one-down strategy might be illustrated in Scripture. But if the Hebrew culture was in any sense a shame culture, as several authors suggest, we have some liberty to guess.[5]

Abram. Abram (not yet called Abraham at this time) may have used a variation of the one-down position in the conflict between his herdsmen and Lot's: "Let's not have any quarreling between you and me, or between your herdsmen and mine, for we are brothers" (Gen 13:8); Abram then offered Lot first pick of the land. Was it simply goodwill Abram wanted, or did he want to avoid bringing shame to the family name? Since Abram did not have real need, and both he and Lot apparently were already wealthy, Lot was quite free to act in his self-interest—a characteristic of human nature that transcends times, cultures and circumstances. Nonetheless, Abram's tactic avoided messy negotiations, preserved the relationship and kept shame from befalling the family name.

Although Lot got the advantage in his settlement with Abram, he soon fell into a one-down position by being captured when the city of Sodom was overthrown by a consortium of kings led by Kedorlaomer (Gen

14:5-12). He was in captivity with his family, and his wealth was gone. Humiliation entered the life of the strong.

Word came to Abram of Lot's vulnerability. Abram responded to Lot's one-down position by raising an army and rescuing Lot and family as well as their wealth (Gen 14:13-20).

After all this, it seems significant that Abram appeals to God out of his own vulnerability. From his one-down position he cries out, "O Sovereign LORD, what can you give me since I remain childless and the one who will inherit my estate is Eliezer of Damascus? . . . You have given me no children; so a servant in my household will be my heir." Abram has been blessed in every way except one. But that need represented one of the greatest humiliations in his culture: to lack a son to perpetuate the family name.

God assured Abram that his days of childless shame would soon be over. He took Abraham outside his tent and told him, "Look up at the heavens and count the stars. . . . So shall your offspring be" (Gen 15:2-5).

David. When David was alienated from his beloved son Absalom, Joab decided to take upon himself the role of mediator (as I mentioned in the last chapter). But he employed the services of a second mediator, a "wise woman" from Tekoa. Joab provided her with the script for her appearance before King David. Noteworthy in that script are the words "Help me, O king!" (2 Sam 14:1-4). Was this cry of vulnerability a cultural use of the one-down position to bring the king into a frame of mind in which he would repeal the law banishing Absalom? It is hard to be certain, but given the nature of Hebrew culture, this is one possible interpretation.

Further, consider the use of a story/parable to arrest David's attention. It would appear that Joab is using every possible indirect means (mediator, one-down and storytelling) to reconcile David and Absalom. But it is naive to believe that father-son reconciliation was Joab's sole purpose. Biblical scholars suggest he was also attempting to carry out a political and personal agenda that depended on the reunion of the king and his son.

Summary

The one-down position is another effective strategy for managing conflict in cultures where avoiding shame, saving face and preserving honor are underlying values. This strategy can be used in a wide variety of situations, and when it is applied appropriately to a given culture, the astute person can be well served. Certain variations of this strategy raise serious biblical questions, but on the whole it does not seem to violate biblical values.

7

STORYTELLING AND PROVERBS

You will not see an elephant moving on your own
head, only the louse moving on another's.
AFRICAN PROVERB

Storytelling is the third indirect means for handling conflict in the
Two-Thirds World. "Storytelling" in this sense is not simply the use
of stories but, in a broader sense, the instructional, corrective and
nuanced use of words. Thus storytelling includes parables, legends,
fables, proverbs, forms of role-play, allegory and, of course, stories.
These various means frequently serve to socialize the younger members
of a society into the norms and values of that society. Yet these same
tools are easily crafted into responses in conflict situations.

When someone violates the standards of a family or a society, or when
someone is heading in a direction that will create a problem, a leader or
wise elderly person may pay a visit to the wayward person. Rather than
dealing directly with the problem, the wise person will enter into social
discourse and at some point, when it seems quite natural, tell a story that
indirectly deals with the problem situation. The hearer understands that

the visit by this person is not just a social call. He or she immediately becomes alert to the hidden message that will surely come in some subtle form during the course of the visit. This strategy was mastered by Jesus in his relationship with the Pharisees.

Among the Bantu in Africa, the storyteller begins with "Are you ready to listen?" The listeners respond with "Yes, we are ready to listen." Storytelling is a refined and sophisticated art, part of an intricate oral tradition, used to instruct, socialize, confront and direct. The African takes seriously the telling of a story. The storyteller might well ask the Westerner who wishes to enter the local culture, "Are you ready to listen?"

The Nigerian Administrator's Story

In a Nigerian hospital, over a period of several weeks, money was consistently missing from one of the three collection points. The hospital's administrator knew which cash till was short and who was responsible for that till. There was no doubt as to the fact of theft and the identity of the thief.

A Westerner's natural reaction would have been to speak to the offender privately and lay out the indisputable facts. There also would have been an attempt to restore the repentant one to good moral standing, perhaps even another job handling money after an appropriate probation. But in much of the Two-Thirds World conflict just does not play this way. Direct face-to-face confrontation with the offender not only would have brought undesirable results but probably would have precipitated other serious problems. So what should the administrator do?

At the regular early-morning meeting with Nigerian and Western medical staff, the administrator explained the problem and the evidence accumulated against the offender. He asked for the thoughts of his colleagues. Several suggested that the offender be confronted with the evidence and put through a process of repentance and restoration. The administrator thanked them for their suggestions, but before departing for the brief daily meeting with the entire hospital staff, he said that on this occasion he would handle the problem the Nigerian way.

At the staff meeting, the administrator proceeded to tell a story. It was set in a village where the people were happy, well fed and secure from their enemies. The children were strong and cheerful. The women sang as they went about their work. The men got along well with each other. Each day was good. With hard work the crops came in abundance. Anger, crying, illness, sadness and discord were infrequent visitors to this peaceful village.

One day, however, a villager became dissatisfied with the amount of food he had, though he had enough to live comfortably and feed his family. He looked at his neighbor's large supply of yams—more yams than that family would need. If he were to take a few yams from their supply, which they would not need anyway, he would not need to work quite so hard. In the darkness of night he took only a few, so that no one would notice that any were missing. He found it rather easy and decided to steal from another person, then another. Soon he had more free time to spend in the shade than anyone else, but still he had as many yams as the others.

Before long others caught on, and they too began stealing. Now the villagers had to find ways of protecting their yams from the thieves. No longer could the people trust each other. They began to fight among themselves. Peace and happiness became strangers to the village; instead it was filled with angry shouting, quarreling, crying, pain and suspicion.

On the opposite hillside was another village. Soon these hill people noticed that it had been some time since they had heard singing from the neighboring village. Eventually they heard the arguments and saw the violence that people do to each other when trust has broken down and friends become adversaries. The villagers on the hillside listened and watched more intently. They knew an opportunity was approaching.

One day, aware that weakness had overtaken the first village, the hillside people swooped down and conquered them. Now there was no happiness, no bounty, no singing, no peace, no freedom for this village that had once enjoyed everything that was important to a good life.

End of story.

The hospital staff who heard the brief story knew that something was amiss. The thief knew he had been discovered, but since nothing specific was said, no one was shamed. The story also served notice to anyone who might be thinking of stealing that they had better think twice.

The thief stopped his stealing, and nothing more was said or done. Had he not stopped, he probably would have been reassigned to a job where he did not come in contact with money—yet still without any overt reference to his misdeeds.

Will the Snake Live Again?

Recently a conference conducted by two friends in Ethiopia yielded a choice illustration of indirect confrontation through storytelling. The conference included missionaries from a U.S.-based agency and their counterparts from the Ethiopian church. All had gone well until, near the close of the conference, a heated debate erupted, threatening the unity and general goodwill of the two groups. The controversy centered on issues of control and submission.

The discussion became more intense. Soon things had deteriorated to the point of collapse as Westerners and Ethiopians traded accusatory statements based on past perceptions and experiences. The unity with the church in Ethiopia was clearly in jeopardy.

At this point, an Ethiopian leader who had been fairly quiet until this point began to tell a story.

As you read the story, put yourself in the position of those listening at the conference. What is the person saying? What does it mean? For whom is it intended? Was he speaking for all Ethiopians at the conference?

I would like to tell a story. A father and his son set out on a journey. Halfway to the point of destination, they encountered a dead snake lying across their path. The father said to his son, "You must tell me with complete honesty your deepest desire, and I will tell you mine. If the truth is told, the snake will come back to life and we will be able to complete our journey."

The father began by saying that his desire was to pass his inheritance on to his son. The son stated, "It is my desire that your desire be fulfilled."

At that moment the snake came back to life and moved off the trail. The two travelers were free to continue on their journey.[1]

Think about the story and its meaning. Here are some observations.

Direct confrontation had brought tensions to a boiling point, and a story (indirect confrontation) was used to give everyone pause to think.

The two parties who had been traveling together were the missionaries and the national church. The snake represented a critical juncture, a crisis, in the journey: would they continue the journey together or go their separate ways? It was a crisis of relationship. It was a time to confront the truth.

The story represents a plea for honesty. The determining factor in a continued relationship was whether each party would tell the truth and be honest with each other. "Tell me your deepest desires, and I will tell you mine." What is your agenda? What are your desires? What do you fear? Can we be honest? In the meeting it had been noted that both sides were being less than honest and each had lost trust in the other. Without trust, how could they continue to work together? Trust could be restored by mutual honesty. In the story it was necessary that both the father and son had to be honest. Honesty must be reciprocal.

The new life of the snake and its apparent departure from the road symbolized hope (new life) for the relationship and a continued walk together down the same road.

The issue of inheritance was brought up. The national church was yearning for independence. This was probably a request not only for the blessing of the mission but also for its "inheritance."

The storyteller had no doubt been listening to his Ethiopian colleagues and foreseen what direction the conference would take. Being a fairly quiet person and perhaps uncomfortable with direct confrontation, he chose to summarize the entire problem with an amazingly simple but powerful story. It ingeniously touched upon all the pieces of the problem that required resolution if the two sides were to enjoy a happy future together.

Proverbs

Proverbs serve as useful indirect means of handling conflict because of their oblique and suggestive character. The speaker wishes to convey something, but in such a way that later on he can deny that he actually stated what was implied, or so that only some among his listeners may understand the point. Proverbs can occur in very many different kinds of contexts; they seem to be particularly important in situations where there is both conflict and, at the same time, some obligation that this conflict should not take on too open and personal a form.[2]

Collectively a group's proverbs summarize its philosophy, and individually they delineate specific values central to a culture. Because proverbs are oblique or, as R. Finnegan says, "elliptical" speech, they are especially effective tools for diffusing latent and hidden tensions. In essence, they "impose a kind of veil which prevents direct confrontation and effectively controls relationships."[3]

Don't Run with the Lions

A friend was a high-level administrator of a hospital in the Middle East. From all appearances the job was going well. One day, as he was going to a higher administrator's office, his immediate supervisor was coming out of that office. As they passed, the supervisor said to him, "If you run with the lions, they will not eat you; but if you do not run with the lions, they will eat you."

My friend found this curious. but because other things were pressing on his mind, he forgot it. A few days later he was fired. Suddenly the proverb made sense to him. His supervisor was telling him that he was not on the inside with the power people and therefore danger lay ahead.

Below are some proverbs from various parts of the world, followed by a mixed-up set of interpretations. See if you can match each of them with its interpretation. Put the appropriate letter in the space provided. See if you can think of a conflict situation in which someone might use any of these proverbs to make a point indirectly and thus defuse a conflict.

Proverbs

1. _____ Seeking a bone in an egg. (China)
2. _____ Even if a log remains in the river for a hundred years, it will never become a crocodile. (Mali)
3. _____ Do not count the eggs until the chicken has laid them. (Brazil)
4. _____ The cat knows, and the rat knows, so the corn stays there. (Haiti)
5. _____ The taller a bamboo grows, the nearer the top bends down to the ground. (Chin people of Burma)
6. _____ A wife is a knife that cuts the life. But there is no life without a wife. (India)
7. _____ He who sleeps with children will wake up wet [from bed-wetting]. (Latin America)
8. _____ It takes two thumbs to squash a louse. (Africa)
9. _____ Big waves are underneath the boat; bit by bit, mountains are underneath the feet. (Burma)
10. _____ The mother of success is failure. (Korea)
11. _____ The short way takes longer. (Japan)
12. _____ Mr. Didn't-Know took shelter from the rain in the pond. (Africa)

13. _____ The rump of the visitor is made to sit upon. (Africa)

14. _____ If a boy says he wants to tie water with a string, ask him if he means the water in the pot or the water in the lagoon. (Africa)

15. _____ There is no blessing for those in a hurry. (Kenya)

16. _____ To the skinny dog the fleas stick. (Nicaragua)

Interpretations

a. Sons want to marry, even if they must then leave their mother's care.

b. One who is speaking foolishly.

c. Learn from your mistakes.

d. Only through cooperation will the job get done. Without cooperation the problem will get worse.

e. Big problems can be conquered one step at a time.

f. Be careful about unrealistic expectations; do not base plans on an unknown.

g. The greater a person is, the more humble the person will be.

h. Someone who is acting foolishly.

i. If you do something in partnership with an immature person, you must be ready to pay the consequences.

j. Always finding fault in another even if there is no fault there.

k. Be sure you know what you are doing if you choose a shortcut.

l. Some students will never become scholars.

m. Equivalent to "Stop and smell the roses": busyness is not a virtue.

n. As long as two rivals are suspicious of each other, they will not cause any damage.

o. Trouble follows trouble; when it rains it pours.

p. Hospitality is an important virtue.

Answers: 1-j; 2-l; 3-f; 4-n; 5-g; 6-a; 7-i; 8-d; 9-e; 10-c; 11-k; 12-h; 13-p; 14-b; 15-m; 16-o.

While the Western reader may not catch the full impact of these proverbs, it is easy to see the power of the well-placed word for putting things in perspective, reducing tension or defusing a conflict-laden situation. None of this, obviously, denies the powerful and positive didactic role played by stories, legends and parables.

Within Biblical Guidelines

A lengthy Old Testament book is dedicated to proverbs, stories and various forms of pithy sayings all designed to help one pursue wisdom over folly. Such pursuit brings happiness, longevity, peace, honor and wealth (Prov 3:13-18) and allows one to avoid the problems, conflicts, tensions and heartaches of the fool (Prov 1:24-33).

Jesus used proverbs to stir thought about treasures in heaven (Mt 6:21), to respond to the scrutiny of the synagogue crowd (Lk 4:23) and to predict his death (Jn 12:24).

Parables and allegories (sometimes the line distinguishing these two forms is not easily drawn) abound in both the Old and New Testaments. Nathan effectively used a story in dealing with King David. David had committed adultery with Bathsheba and had gotten her pregnant. Having seen to it that her husband Uriah was killed in battle, David covered up the adultery and took Bathsheba for himself. In his prophetic role, Nathan told David a story; but the king failed to catch the point until Nathan, no doubt at great personal risk, became direct in his words: "You are the man" (2 Sam 12:1-9).

One might suggest that Pharaoh's dreams were given in the form of allegory or parable, for which Joseph was able to discern the hidden meaning, thus positioning himself to fulfill God's purposes in Egypt. In the ancient Near East, anyone adept at interpreting puzzling situations was honored as a wise person.

In 2 Samuel 14 Joab crafts a story for Tekoa, noted as a wise woman, to tell King David so that he will think about the conflict with his son Absalom and become willing to bring him back to Jerusalem for the good of all Israel.

Matthew 21 records two situations in which indirect methods were used. One was a puzzle and the other a parable. The puzzle grew out of the question from the chief priests and elders to Jesus: "By what authority are you doing these things?"

Jesus answered with a question/puzzle: "John's baptism—where did it come from? Was it from heaven, or from men?"

If Jesus' would-be accusers answered "From heaven," they knew Jesus would say, "Then why didn't you believe him?" But if they answered "From men," they would have reason to fear the common people, who widely considered John to be a prophet. So they said the only safe thing: "We don't know."

Jesus responded, "Neither will I tell you by what authority I am doing these things" (vv. 23-27). Jesus' indirect tactic provided an effective means for avoiding a potentially explosive situation.

Just a few verses later, Jesus tells a parable about a landowner who planted a lovely vineyard and rented it to some farmers to tend. The landowner went on a long journey but sent servants to "collect his fruit." The tenants treated the servants badly, even killing one, and sent them away. The owner sent another delegation with similar results. So finally the owner sent his own son, assuming they would respect him. But alas, the son was killed too.

Then Jesus posed a question to further draw in his listeners: "When the owner of the vineyard comes, what will he do to those tenants?"

The audience quickly responded, "He will bring those wretches to a wretched end."

Jesus made some further application but did not directly state who was the intended target of this parable. Yet the message arrived at its hoped-for destination: "When the chief priests and the Pharisees heard Jesus' parables, they knew he was talking about them." Unfortunately, the parable did not bring them to repentance. Instead the chief priests and Pharisees "looked for a way to arrest him" (vv. 33-46).

When the Pharisees were grumbling about Jesus' unorthodox ways, he responded with the parables of the lost sheep, the lost coin and the lost (prodigal) son (Lk 15). When the arrogant, self-righteous leaders were looking down their noses on the ordinary people, Jesus chose a story as an indirect means of confronting them with their pride.

Two men went up to the temple to pray, one a Pharisee and the other a tax collector. The Pharisee stood up and prayed about himself: "God, I thank you that I am not like other men—robbers, evildoers, adulterers—or even like this tax collector. I fast twice a week and give a tenth of all I get."

But the tax collector stood at a distance. He would not even look up to heaven, but beat his breast and said, "God, have mercy on me, a sinner."

I tell you that this man, rather than the other, went home justified before God. For everyone who exalts himself will be humbled, and he who humbles himself will be exalted. (Lk 18:10-14)

Notice that Jesus spoke of the two people in terms of their occupational categories: Pharisee and tax collector. He obviously wanted to make sure that at least the Pharisees would not miss the point.

Clearly, it was perfectly acceptable to become more direct if one's point was either missed or ignored. This was especially true when the most important issues—like eternal life—were at stake. The same holds true in Two-Thirds World societies today.

Hebrew culture utilized the indirect method of handling conflict by the use of proverbs, stories, allegories and parables. But the indirectness did not make this way of dealing with conflict less effective; in fact, quite probably the opposite was true. Indeed, it was the gospel of God in Christ—God working indirectly through his incarnated Son—that captured people's hearts. Other means would have been insensitive and culturally offensive to any whose ear was tuned to hear.

Summary

Telling parables, stories, folktales or allegories can be a useful indirect strategy for confronting people in conflict situations without risking their loss of face or shame. Typically these methods are effective in resolving problems. When they are not, more specificity or directness can be employed. Of course this increases the possibility of a negative reaction, but when the issue is particularly important, the risk may be worthwhile. The Scripture generally supports this indirect approach, but not necessarily in every way it is used in a given culture.

8
INACTION, MISDIRECTION, SILENCE AND INDEFINITE PERSONS

He who knows much speaks with silence.
AMHARIC PROVERB

A church in South Africa was struggling financially. Its building was quite nice, the monthly payments were very small, and there were few other expenses except for the pastor's salary. The attendance was reasonably good, and because the country's economy was strong at the time, nearly everyone was employed. Yet there never seemed to be enough money in the offering to meet the pastor's salary, which had been set by the church leadership. The pastor occasionally mentioned to me that sometimes there was not enough money to buy food. His house and car suggested that he was not prospering. As a new missionary, I was confused, because from all appearances there should have been enough income from the congregation.

My guess now is that the congregation had not found a good fit between themselves and the pastor. Rather than dealing with the issue directly, they communicated their feelings about the pastor by withholding much of their financial support to the church.

Ideally with such a strategy, the pastor would soon get the message and begin to think about finding a different place of ministry. This pastor, however, stayed on for a number of years. Often he would receive subsidies from either the mission agency associated with the church or from individual missionaries. While this help was undoubtedly motivated by generosity, perhaps it actually worked at cross-purposes with the congregation and only postponed the inevitable.

If non-Western pastors have been trained in the West or a Western-style school, they may tend to lose their cultural sensitivities and, in some cases, even reject them. Having adopted Western ways, they may no longer be on the same wavelength as their congregation. In such instances, indirect messages may be understood by neither the local pastor nor the missionary.

Often a missionary or mission will provide a percentage of a pastor's salary in the early years of a church's planting, continuing until the church is large enough to carry the full support. The missionary may even have been instrumental in placing the pastor in the church. The church, not wanting to cause the missionary loss of face, accepts the pastor as a courtesy and with measured enthusiasm. But if the pastor is not able to fit in and win the people's support, they will express their feelings by supporting the person only minimally. The Westerner finds this cruel, but it seems an acceptable strategy in a number of places; sometimes it is used even in Western churches!

But one can't automatically assume that if the local congregation cannot support its pastor, it is necessarily in opposition to the person. There might be very legitimate reasons for the lack of funds, and extra help may be most welcome. At the same time, it is a mistake to assume that long-term financial generosity is really what is needed to help a situation. A naive assumption could foster an unhealthy dependency. I am for generosity, but misguided benevolence can cause more damage than good. Generosity is best offered through an informed, wise understanding of cultural values.

Dogs, Chickens and the Postal Service

A Westerner arrived in a Two-Thirds World country and plunged into his new responsibilities. One of his hobbies was hunting, and soon he realized that a few local people had trained dogs to assist in the sport. After searching for some while, he found a suitable canine companion and began enjoying his hobby.

Most houses in the area had walls, but his did not. Thinking the dog would stay within the property lines, however, the Westerner let it run loose.

One day the local postmaster saw him in the post office and humbly asked for his help. A neighborhood dog was chasing his chickens at night, and he was asking people to please help him protect his chickens.

The postmaster expected an expression of concern, but the new expatriate only expressed doubt that it was his dog. Nevertheless, he would tie it up at night.

A few days later, as the Westerner was gathering his mail, the postmaster approached him again, this time more direct and stern. The dog *must* be tied at night, because his chickens were still being killed. Feeling misjudged, the dog owner offered little response; he *had* been tying the dog at night. It eventually came out that only most of the time was the dog still on its leash in the morning. Sometimes it got loose.

For the next several weeks, as the Westerner collected his mail each day, he noticed an obvious coolness from the postal workers toward him. He had always received prompt help when he needed stamps or other services, but now it took much longer. When other people had mail in their boxes, he had none. He began to angrily berate the postal workers for negligence and not providing the service for which they were being paid.

One day the postmaster came out from behind the counter and openly confronted the Westerner. If the dog continued to kill his chickens, he would do something. That night the missionary tied his dog and went to bed. Around midnight he heard what seemed like a shotgun blast from the direction of the post office. Since he did not think it concerned him, he went back to sleep. The next morning he noticed his dog was not there. He called its name several times to no avail. He decided the dog would return in its own time and went off to work.

At the usual time that day he went to pick up his mail, and as he passed the clerks they gave him friendly greetings. The postmaster was unusually kind and warmly inquired about his family, his church and life in general. Not understanding this switch in attitude but happy for it, the Westerner went home rather stunned and amazed.

Later that night, he realized that the shot he had heard was his dog being killed for disturbing the postmaster's chickens. Fortunately, he had the wisdom not to make an issue out of it and went on with his life. Shortly thereafter the postmaster began attending church and became a regular participant.

For the most part, the local people's attitudes toward dogs lay somewhere between tolerance and hostility. Except for those used in hunting, dogs were considered noncontributors to society and not worthy of respect. Chickens, on the other hand, were part of the household economy, providing eggs, meat and income. So chickens were respected and allowed to run free; if you owned a dog, however, it should be tied or otherwise contained at all times. The new Westerner had come from a culture where the opposite attitude existed: dogs could run free and chickens should be locked up, at least at night.

The postal clerks, unhappy with the Westerner's complaints about their poor service, chose to ignore his needs and intentionally delay services to him. This deliberate inaction and neglect were intended to show the Westerner that his behavior was inappropriate—both his criticisms and his failure to show proper respect for other people's property (the chickens). The Westerner, however, saw the neglect as further evidence that the clerks lacked a work ethic.

Both were using conflict management strategies that communicate effectively and *usually work in their respective cultures,* but in this cross-cultural setting the normal strategies served only to compound the problem.[1]

The burden was on the newcomer to learn and adjust, since he was a guest in the country. Once he understood their strategies, he might fully accept and adjust to their ways, partially accept and adjust, or determine that he could not accept and adjust. But such a choice must always be based on an understanding of the local culture and not on one's own cultural values.

Guilt by Association

Lesotho, a small country surrounded by South Africa, drew numerous white South African tourists because of its gambling casino and the women who were available for a "good time." Meanwhile, many Basotho men—natives of Lesotho—could find work only in South Africa's mines. The good income the white South Africans made off the sweat of Basotho men was being used to gamble and encourage prostitution in Lesotho. In some cases the wives of Basotho men were drawn into prostitution while their husbands were in the South African mines. Adding to the embarrassment was the fact that the women who prostituted themselves were making twenty-five or thirty times more money than their mineworker husbands or most other men employed in Lesotho. Some women began to feel and act superior to their male partners, to the consternation of extended family and friends.

Bill, the new missionary, was unaware of the strong negative feelings of Basotho men toward white South Africans. Bill was white, but not South African; but he had South African license plates on his car, since he had ministered there before being transferred to Lesotho. The Basotho people simply assumed he was just another white South African exploiting Basotho men in the mines and Basotho women in their own country.

When Bill went to fill up his car with gas, the attendant failed to "see"

Bill for a full six to eight minutes and then announced, "Oh, I did not see you drive up. What do you want?"

Anyone familiar with this region of the world knows how unlikely it is that a gas attendant would fail to hear a car drive up. Actually, the attendant noticed the license plates of the car and used inaction to signal his displeasure with this person he believed to be a South African. The attendant would fulfill his duty, but not without showing the car owner that he was less than welcome.

In succeeding visits to various shops Bill noticed similar reactions. In one store a group of young men, under the pretense of helping Bill and his family with a door that appeared to be stuck, ended up pushing them all out onto the sidewalk, where they lay in confusion. The youths walked off laughing. No injury had come to Bill or his family. The youths tried to make the shoving seem like an accident, but this misdirection ("helping" but really intending to embarrass) was a more overt attempt to show the young men's disrespect for white South Africans.

At first Bill was tempted to make harsh judgments about Basotho people and their lack of friendliness and courtesy. Their bad manners were in contrast to what he had heard about them. Once he realized they were prejudging him by his license plates and assuming that his white skin meant he was South African, Bill could adjust.

From then on, whenever he went to the shop or gas station he immediately spoke to the clerk or attendant, explained his presence in the country and noted how happy he was to be in this peace-loving land. Recognizing his accent as being non-South African, the people quickly welcomed him with the warmth consistent with their reputation.[2]

Where Is the Lamp?
The following story exemplifies the tactic of misdirection or diverting the blame. When a person cannot fulfill certain obligations, she or he fears loss of face. The person needing to save face leads the other person to believe that the blame is not her or his own. When this happens in the

West, we call it "scapegoating," the placing of blame somewhere else when it is primarily our own fault. In other parts of the world, however, the strategy of "misdirection," "deflection" or "diversion" is a finely honed art. Instead of accepting the responsibility for some problem, one directs, deflects or diverts the blame elsewhere, usually to circumstances or to a lower-status person. Here is how it worked out in the purchase of a lamp.

A foreigner working in the country purchased a large desk lamp from a Chinese merchant. The delivery was promised for the next afternoon. When the foreigner called wondering why the lamp had not been delivered, he was told that the delivery man was sick and the delivery might be in a few days.

When the foreigner said he would be willing to come by and pick it up in person, the manager said that unfortunately there were some workmen nearby repairing the water lines, and the road was most difficult to travel. When asked how serious the delivery man's condition was, the manager said that actually it was the delivery man's sister who was sick, and he was at her bedside. The truth of the matter was that the lamp was out of stock, however the shop manager was embarrassed, or thought it would be a loss of face, to say that. He was trying to stall for time until he could receive delivery of the appropriate lamp from his wholesaler, and the fact that the customer could not infer this from his comments was most surprising.[3]

The merchant wanted to provide efficient service and please the customer. Saying "No, I cannot deliver the lamp tomorrow" would have disappointed the customer, something all merchants wish to avoid, especially in a "face" or shame culture. The foreigner would have preferred a direct, honest answer, even if the bad news was that he would have to wait a few more days. Again, both were operating from their own cultural norms.

Suppose you were in the same situation. Knowing what you know now, what would you do if there was no urgency in having the lamp delivered? On the other hand, what if you very much needed the lamp delivered tomorrow because of a special event at your house? Think about it before reading on.

If there was no urgency, you might wait an extra day and then call again and gently inquire. Getting the message about the sickness, you might assume that the lamp was going to arrive, but not at the specified time. You would not assume deliberate deception or malice.

If it was urgent that the lamp arrive the next day, you might (before purchasing it) say how important it is to have the lamp delivered tomorrow. If it does not arrive, your embarrassment will be great because of the important friends you are expecting. Besides, your friends will want to know where you purchased such a beautiful lamp.

Now the merchant realizes that he might cause you loss of face if the delivery is not made. Understanding the situation, he may (1) suggest that you purchase another lamp (meaning one he has in stock and can deliver at the stated time), (2) offer the use of the floor model until a new lamp can be obtained from the warehouse or (3) try a face-saving way of escape such as "I think this is the perfect lamp for you, but my driver is sick and may not be able to make the delivery."

Westerners prefer direct forms of communication and are not good at reading between the lines. Yet in most cultures the people are masters at indirect speech, and one must become accustomed to it if one is to survive and prosper in the Two-Thirds World. Although at first it seems mystifying and frustrating to be constantly decoding people's speech, it soon becomes second nature, and eventually one finds enjoyment in practicing the new skill.

When Yes Means No: or, the Relational Yes
Particularly in business environments between Westerners and Asians, it is most difficult to know when to take someone literally. For example, the Westerner may ask an Asian to investigate a certain matter and come up with a recommendation. A Westerner receiving the same request

might respond, "I do not have the time, budget or personnel necessary to do that." The Asian, however, might say, "Yes, I will get right on it," though he or she knows that it will not get done.

When the request has not been fulfilled in a reasonable time, the Asian expects the Westerner to infer that the task was too much to be accomplished. Were the Westerner to press the issue, the Asian would experience loss of face, feel unjustly maligned and eventually consider changing jobs.

Although the Westerner made a request, it was interpreted by the Asian as a demand. To have refused would have been to deny a superior her or his request or desire, something an Asian usually resists. Not to fulfill important persons' wishes is to cause them and yourself loss of face. So one is left without option except to say, "Yes, I will get right on it." People of status need to exercise great care in their language. Their carelessness can put others in a position of no option—they must say yes even when they know they cannot fulfill the commitment.

The Westerner might try being more indirect by using a leading statement such as "I imagine the project will be difficult to complete without enough resources." Such a leading statement does not require a yes or no response and gives the other person room to negotiate without losing face or causing loss of face. So he or she can freely respond with "No, I can manage" or "You are right. I think we will need . . ."

I live near Chicago. Some time ago a Vietnamese builder was putting on an addition to my neighbor's house. One day I noticed that the plastic cover on my basement window-well was broken. Since the two houses were close, boards and other debris sometimes were in my yard and near this window-well. It seemed likely that the damage had been unintentionally done by one of the workers. So I decided to talk with the builder.

After complimenting him on the excellent work and talking about the building trade, I pointed out the damaged plastic cover. He agreed that one of his crew might have inadvertently damaged it and said he would replace it for me.

After waiting a couple of weeks, I struck up another conversation with the builder and, in passing, mentioned the cover. Again he promised a replacement. When the addition was nearly completed, our conversation was repeated once again. The cover never did get replaced.

My guess is that the builder did not think his workers had caused the damage but could not tell me so because that would have contradicted my thinking and caused me to lose face. On the other hand, he did not feel responsible for the damage and did not feel obligated to replace the cover. So he used the "relational yes."

I Want to Eat Some Sushi

Recently when my son and I were in Japan, we were picked up at the airport by two delightful young men. They made us feel greatly welcomed and honored. In the course of conversation, they asked my nineteen-year-old son what he was hoping to do while here. His first response was "I want to eat some sushi."

Immediately our two hosts reverted into animated Japanese, the car began to change direction, and before long we arrived at a sushi restaurant. After a twelve-hour nonstop flight from Chicago with what seemed an endless supply of food and little sleep, we were stuffing our stomachs again!

"Your wish is my command" is the motto of the Asian toward the honored guest. My son wisely caught on and changed his language to "Sometime [or later on] during my stay I would like . . ." The Asian desire to please and never say no is very strong. It is up to the guest to adjust accordingly.

Promises and Apologies

Muriel, reared in Africa and now director of several projects in Asia and Latin America, finds the inaction response one of the more difficult to handle. One Peruvian she works with promised to translate a particular document from Spanish into English. The first deadline passed, and he was only half done. Her telephone call to him brought profuse apologies and renewed promises that it would be completed. The second deadline passed, and the story was repeated. A third deadline now approached, and no document had arrived. As far as Muriel was concerned, she would have to cancel the contract and the remaining payment.

She is not sure of the reason for the delay. Is the job harder than he thought and he does not think it worth his effort? Is he unsure of his English and fearful of losing face? Or if his work does not meet expectations, he may cause Muriel to lose face. Have there been emergencies? Did he take the job to please her though he knew he would be too busy to complete it?

The situation remains unresolved. Muriel plans to write to the translator, saying that she managed to get the work done and he should not put any more work into the project. She will not mention payment, since he did not fulfill the contract. If he brings it up, she may negotiate something for his actual time. Knowing about the concepts of shame and "face," Muriel had sensed early on that he might not get the work done, and she wisely made a contingency plan.

In all her communication, she was careful not to say anything that would cause him to lose face. Muriel diligently resisted making a negative judgment about his motives or character. She still does not know why he failed to complete the project, but by knowing some cultural realities, she was able to reduce the frustration and stress that often accompany such situations.

When Silence Is Wisdom

It is wise to take special care in protecting the face of authorities, superiors, elders, teachers, friends and people of stature. Many people in indirect cultures may understand directness and not take offense. But it is better to play it safe and know the rules. If they allow you freedom to be yourself, fine, but even then act with discretion. You will rarely go wrong by showing respect for the traditions of a people. Sometimes this means silence.

Suppose a Two-Thirds World lecturer you are listening to makes a wrong statement—say, that the Declaration of Independence was signed in 1786. You might be tempted to seek an appropriate time to correct the error and set the record straight. But if you choose to do so, even if you exercise great courtesy, the lecturer will lose face and sense great shame because his expertise will have been publicly discredited. Since teachers desire to be competent, and since competence is attached to "face," anyone exposing an error or challenging a point is considered insensitive, rude and ill-mannered. Thus there exists a curious preference in face-saving cultures that it is better to "be all wrong in a harmonious fashion than be all right in a disharmonious fashion."[4] The reasoning goes as follows:

> While the [listener's] statement of these dates is more accurate historically, yet by causing the professor to lose face he has caused disharmony in the learning environment. This has created disrespect. How can a teacher teach without respect? Hence, it can be seen that the concept of respect is also very closely related to face: to the extent that you can keep up an image, even though it may be a false one, in front of a group, you have face. If you lose this image, you have lost face.[5]

In cases where an expert, superior or some respected member of society has committed some error of fact or judgment, it might be wise to keep silent. Correctness and precision are Western values, but in many situations relationship may be more important than accuracy. Of course, if the issue had to do with landing an airplane or performing triple bypass surgery, most of us would opt for pinpoint accuracy over a good relationship. Keep in mind, though, that most situations are not life-and-death matters.

In negotiations, such as a business deal, numbers and accuracy may be crucial. If someone who may be sensitive to shame makes an error and the negotiations cannot be completed until it is set right, you might try the following: "I am so sorry that I do not have all the facts clearly in my mind and I must waste your time, but could we go back in the documents and look for some things that are causing me some confusion?" Such a statement does not place blame, point out error or suggest fault. You put the blame on yourself (one-down) and ask for the other's indulgence. As you look through the documents, you note several places where the numbers agree and then "happen upon" those that do not agree.

To the Westerner this approach seems like playing games, but those in other cultures will consider you wise, a person to be trusted and respected.

Visiting, Inviting and Disappointment

I encountered frequent frustration in my community-visitation and church-planting efforts. After drinking tea and talking with a family, I would invite them to a Bible study or church service. They would assure me that they would be at the meeting, send their children to Sunday school, attend church or whatever. But by my estimate, 98 percent of the time or more they did not show. I could understand that some would have emergencies, but that would only account for a few. The others, it appeared to me, had blatantly lied. They said one thing but never intended to come—the relational yes.

On numerous occasions I would go back to the family. I would express my disappointment at not seeing them at the meeting, and they would always offer a reason: my car was broken, my daughter was ill, my sister visited and so on—misdirection or diversion. Often they would promise to come next time, only to disappoint me again. While I found their excuses hard to accept, I expect I brought it on myself.

My mistake was in seeking some kind of accountability for their absence. They had no intention of coming, yet to save face they said they would. Then when I asked "Why?" they had to invent a reason or be exposed and lose face.

Had I been wiser, I might have given them a general invitation, not a specific one, so they would not be forced to say yes but mean no. Second, when I tried to follow up, I would never have needed to express disappointment or inquire as to their absence. I could have simply continued showing interest in them without calling for some definite commitment. In this way their "face" would not have been questioned and they would have felt much better about me.

Westerners tend to interpret responses like those above as deceitful or dishonest. "However, in cross-cultural interchanges such a classification is not always so readily applicable. . . . When one's remarks are made without deliberate intent to cheat, defraud, or physically harm, they are essentially outside of the honesty/dishonesty spectrum."[6] So it is better to see them for what they are: attempts to save face, not to defraud or do harm.

One could argue that Westerners have their own culturally acceptable lies. For example, are you always completely honest when someone asks, "How do you like the new painting on our wall?" or when your boss says, "What do you think of my new coat?" or when the pastor asks, "What did you think of the sermon this morning?" Frequently the Westerner will be less than honest in an attempt not to hurt the feelings of the other person. These so-called white lies are not meant to deceive or injure but to protect and maintain a relationship.

There are some, however, who insist on complete and forthright honesty regardless of the cultural context. "Let your yea be yea and your nay be nay" is their biblical support. Yet as we have already observed, biblical support for one position does not necessarily deny biblical support for a different one. More study is needed both in the Scriptures and in cultures. Such study should be carried out by mature, astute Christians from a variety of cultures.

Goats Versus People

In Java, Indonesia, some people instituted a goat-raising project. At one point the project director took a male goat as his own private possession. The other leaders in the project were aware of the problem. When they met, they talked about the missing goat without mentioning the person's name. Furthermore, when they spoke of the problem they used the most respectful of the three levels of the local language to show the highest respect for the person.

During the deliberation, an educated and esteemed woman addressed the problem, also using the highest level of Javanese. Using the highest level of Javanese served to give face to the problem person. No direct accusations were made, and the spirit of the speech was noticeably nonjudgmental. In these situations what is not said is often as important as what is said, or even more important.

If the project director gave the goat back, it would constitute admission of guilt and expose him to open shame. If he were confronted and forced to return the goat, it would be a serious loss of face. In either case only one option would remain open to him: leave the community. In the best scenario he would leave alone or with his immediate family. In the worst scenario he would try to take as many people as possible with him. Regardless, not only would he be shamed, but so would his entire extended family and network of friends. So much was at stake that an admission of guilt was highly unlikely.

In other cultures the person might not leave the community but might launch a smear campaign on the accusers. If one has been openly shamed, one recourse is to retaliate by heaping greater shame on those who brought the shame. These situations become incredibly messy and usually end up with people in adversarial camps.

In Western cultures truth, honesty and justice are of greater value than the individual and relationship. The guilty party or parties must be specifically identified and punished and must make restitution. In many countries outside the West, however, values of precision, blame and repayment are of lesser importance. The people would rather lose a goat than a person.

The solution? The group determined that the project should buy another male goat. What about the offender? They would assume that there must be good reason for him to take the goat. He would know that it had caused considerable concern. He would also know that further violations could bring him public shame. All hoped that he had learned his lesson and would direct his affairs more uprightly in the future.

In some places, the shame factor is breaking down with greater exposure to Western ways. As the stigma of shame becomes less intense, confession and restitution become viable options. The Spirit of God is working to bring the church into conformity with the Scriptures. Meanwhile Western Christians need to be patient, enter into open-minded discussion of the cultural expressions of key Scriptures and make sure they do not impose Western ways simply because they are more comfortable. On the other hand, the fact that something is a cultural value does not make it right. No one culture has exclusive claim on the truth. But as we pray, exercise humility and search the Scriptures together, the Spirit of God will lead us into truth. Then if confrontation seems necessary, let it be done with understanding, love and a gentle spirit.

Beyond Goats

We are not told why the leader stole the goat. However, sometimes a relatively minor but blatant social violation is committed in order to provoke an open discussion. In open discussion the normal rules are suspended, to a degree. One may bring up another grievance—usually the real issue and the more important one—which could not have been addressed earlier by other methods. Thus the stealing of a goat may only have been a tactic to generate open discussion during which the leader now could air the real grievance.

What might the real grievance have been? Perhaps the leader was dissatisfied with the committee's functioning, poor pay for his work or lack of respect from a committee member. Perhaps he wanted to get out of the leadership role but did not know how. There are any number of other possible reasons.

In any event, some conflicts are intentional and designed to force the real issue to be addressed. In these situations the Westerner rarely knows the culture well enough to accurately judge whether an issue should be brought to an open forum or be dealt with more indirectly. Careful conversation with a wise local person may be the best way to proceed in such circumstances.

I Will Speak to This Leg

The use of the indefinite person, sometimes called a third party, is the last of the indirect strategies. The Westerner may use a form of this strategy, but never with the sophistication found in the Two-Thirds World.

In the film *Out of Africa,* a young Kikuyu lad of about eleven or twelve comes to the coffee-plantation owner. He approaches the baroness on crutches because of the infected gash on his leg. Other adults stand around watching. She crouches to be at eye level with him, showing both respect and interest in his words. He looks down at the ground, signaling his respect for an elder. Noticing the infected leg, she says, "You must go to the hospital."

The lad says, "This leg may be foolish. It think it not go to hospital."

She responds, "This leg will do as it pleases. If you will take it to hospital, I will think that you are wise. And such a wise man as this I would want to work in my house for wages."

"How much wages would come to such a wise man as that?" he answers.

"More wages than come from tending goats," she says.

"I will speak to this leg" are his final words as he turns to leave.

The baroness's first instruction is direct: "You must go to the hospital." Her directness implies that the boy has been negligent, which immediately raises the issue of shame for not having acted wisely. The lad, to save face, disassociates himself, his person, from his leg: "This leg may be foolish." The leg may be talked about as though it were a separate entity, an indefinite third party.

The baroness wisely picks up the cue and speaks of the leg as independent of the person. By introducing the idea of what a wise person would do, she allows the boy to leave with face and dignity intact. He eventually does come to work for her.

A variation of this strategy is when negative human characteristics are attributed to inanimate objects. For example, instead of saying that someone is lazy, one might say that the person has a "weak machete and hoe."[7] The message is the same, but the latter method shields the lazy party from the direct, blunt truth. Responsibility for work undone is placed on the "weak" machete and hoe, not on the person.

Bad Air
The need to be indefinite is expressed differently in the next illustration. In this scenario there is no escaping the placing of blame, because the group is small and any complaint could only be seen as placing blame. In such situations one may resort to intangibles such as "bad air" to carry the responsibility for the problem.

> An elderly woman admitted to a hospital against her wishes was required to take daily showers after the acute phase of her illness was past. She objected, since her custom was less frequent baths, but her objections were ignored. While returning from her shower shortly thereafter she had an attack of "bad air," a folk-defined illness, which in her opinion, and that of her family, was the result of the dangerous practice of daily showers. The illness gained her the sympathy of her family, who caused her to be released prematurely to be taken home for what they felt was the proper care.[8]

The woman was in a bind. To have made any complaint about the hospital would have placed blame on the staff. So "bad air" became the intangible culprit. The "bad air" became the third party or mediator that allowed a conflict to be resolved without anyone being shamed. In this situation the mediator was the environment rather than a person—a very nonconfrontational, nonshaming but creative way of responding to a conflict.

Can a Person Date?

Recently, while teaching in New Haven, Connecticut, I looked up a former student of mine who was now studying at Yale Divinity School. After a meal and a lovely drive around the area, he took me to the top of a bluff that overlooked the beautiful city. He began probing my thoughts about the issue of a church's staff member dating and perhaps getting serious about a member of the congregation. Is it acceptable for a person to do this? What are the implications? If it were done, when should the dating relationship be made public? If it is made public, should the staff member leave the position? He had many questions.

I assumed he had discovered this situation in his church and was trying to get some perspective on it. I failed to catch on, partly because I did not know he was working in a church and partly because I was not expecting an indirect strategy from this long-standing friend.

But this Korean friend was being very Korean. He was the leader of a college group and had dated one of the group members, but was not sure how a staff member should conduct himself in such situations. It was especially burdensome because he thought the relationship had long-term potential and, now in his mid-twenties, he had to be thinking marriage. His use of the indefinite third person was, I suspect, a form of protection until he determined my attitude. Since I explored the question in a nonjudgmental way, eventually he seemed to feel comfortable giving me the personal details. We talked it through. He seemed at peace, and I felt greatly honored.

The student-teacher distinction so carefully maintained by Koreans had now become a colleague-friend relationship. I was refreshed in believing that in some mysterious and wonderful way he and I had fulfilled 1 Corinthians 12:12: "The body is a unit, though it is made up of many parts; and though all its parts are many, they form one body. So it is with Christ."

Within Biblical Guidelines?

The following story raises questions about the difference between deception and a culturally acceptable strategy: The first chapter of Exodus tells us that a new king "who did not know about Joseph" (v. 8) came to power in Egypt. The king looked around the land and noticed that "the Israelites have become much too numerous for us" (v. 9). A plan was crafted to decrease the Israelite population. Part of the plan involved two Hebrew midwives, Shiphrah and Puah, who were instructed to kill each Hebrew boy at birth but allow the girl babies to live.

The midwives feared God and "did not do what the king of Egypt told them to do" (v. 17). Eventually the king called the two women in and asks them why they had been letting the male babies live. They responded, "Hebrew women are not like Egyptian women; they are vigorous and give birth before the midwives arrive" (v. 19).

In this brief story that sets the scene for Moses' birth, we have a serious conflict of interests and, in a larger sense, a conflict between the forces of good and the forces of evil. The Hebrew midwives used several strategies in managing this conflict: silence (they did not reply to the king's request), inaction (they did not do as he had commanded) and misdirection/diversion (they placed blame elsewhere—on the Hebrew women who gave birth before they could arrive).

Western Christians are both pleased and troubled by this story. They would affirm the women for choosing not to obey the king because they feared God. Some are troubled, however, that the midwives remained silent before the king and did not "speak the truth" of their convictions and tell him outright that they would not obey. Perhaps most troubling is the blatant, self-serving "lie" the midwives told regarding the Hebrew women's delivering the children before they arrived.

Adding to our confusion are the words immediately following, in which God reveals his commentary on the series of events: "So God was kind to the midwives" (v. 20). God seems to have approved (at least he did not judge or condemn) the silence and the "lie." Perhaps these tactics were understood differently than we understand them and need to be further understood so we can see them as God does.

The New King Remains Silent

Samuel brought Saul before the people as God's anointed king. He was received well by the masses, but, as often is the case, there were some troublemakers who said, "How can this fellow save us?" To show their spite for the new king, they "brought him no gifts" (1 Sam 10:27). The troublemakers were experiencing conflict and used the indirect method of inaction to show their displeasure. No words were spoken, but the message was very clear to all present. Yet if someone accused them of not giving proper honor to the king, they could make excuses in an attempt to hide their public shame.

Of further interest is Saul's response. He could, as king, have had them punished or killed for indirectly embarrassing him. Instead, the same verse says, "Saul kept silent."

Silence does not mean the issue is settled or that some agreement has been reached. It usually means a delay until another appropriate strategy can be employed.

Several other passages further illustrate these points. In Psalm 4:4 David realizes that in a conflict with God there comes a time to "be silent" and search one's heart. In Isaiah 18:4-6, when Cush is going to be destroyed, God remains quiet and watches from a distance—inaction and silence. Would Cush get the message? Rahab's deliberate misleading of the men who had come to capture the two spies can be seen as misdirection or diversion, a culturally appropriate way of handling conflict. God added his commendation later (see Heb 11:31).

Breaking Silence

Esther had remained silent before the king with regard to the abuse of the Jews. But then Mordecai uncovered Haman's plot to destroy them and made it known to Esther. She realized that if the king was not kindly disposed to her concern for her people, she would lose not only her throne but her life as well. Knowing this, she called for prayer and fasting (Esther 4). The king realized that something was troubling her and asked for her petition (5:3). She felt that silence was best for the moment. The time would come to speak, to be direct, to confront, to lay it on the line.

Esther prepared a banquet to which Haman and the king were invited (5:4). There the king renewed his request to hear her petition; again she demurred and asked him to come with Haman to a second banquet (5:6-8).

At the second feast, the king asked once more what she would seek from him. Then Queen Esther answered, "If I have found favor with you, O king, and if it pleases your majesty, grant me my life—this is my petition. And spare my people—this is my request. For I and my people have been sold for destruction and slaughter and annihilation. If we had merely been sold as male and female slaves, I would have kept quiet, because no such distress would justify disturbing the king" (7:3-4).

There is a time for silence and a time for forthrightness. It seems that the gravity of the issue is one indicator for choosing, as is timeliness. Notice two additional characteristics of Esther's response: she used the passive voice, and she did not directly accuse Haman.

Indirectness in the New Testament

Mark 9:33-37 tells how Jesus asked the disciples what they had been talking about as they journeyed together. Since they had been debating who would be the greatest in the kingdom, they felt caught and "kept quiet": to have confessed would have been to expose their shame. Jesus, rather than condemning them for what they had been discussing, presents them with a paradox—"If anyone wants to be first, he must be the very last, and the servant of all"—and a sort of object lesson, bringing a child to stand among them. Jesus does not expose their shame directly, but addresses the problem and provides them with higher ideals.

Jesus' handling of the woman taken in adultery (Jn 8:1-11) may reveal several indirect strategies. The Pharisees and teachers of the law were often trying to lay a trap by which they could discredit (shame) him so the people would not follow him. They brought him an adulterous woman and said, "In the Law Moses commanded us to stone such women. Now what do you say?" (v. 5).

Jesus remained silent but wrote on the ground as they were continuing their questioning. Then his simple statement "If any one of you is without sin, let him be the first to throw a stone at her" disarmed the accusers, who departed in chagrin. Did Jesus use misdirection to solve this conflict—diverting the focus from the woman's sin to their own?

In the hours leading up to the cross, after Jesus' accusers presented their charges against him, Pilate asked for Jesus' response. "But Jesus made no reply, not even to a single charge—to the great amazement of the governor" (Mt 27:14). Silence can be its own form of judgment.

Summary

Two-Thirds World people may use inaction, silence, misdirection and the indefinite third party as means of handling conflict situations. To the Westerner such strategies may appear at times ethically questionable; but that may not necessarily be the case. We must understand what lying and deception are in that particular culture and weigh that against Scripture. The Bible does not overtly condemn these indirect strategies; in several situations it seems to support their use.

Bringing a cultural practice under the authority of Scripture is not Westerners' exclusive responsibility. All of us are prone to interpret the Bible through our cultural lenses and to mingle our own cultural preferences with biblical teaching. Christians from various cultures would serve one another and the cause of biblical interpretation by joining in prayer and discussion on these matters.

PART 3

IMPLICATIONS FOR THE GOSPEL MESSAGE

9

COMMUNICATING THE GOSPEL ACROSS CULTURES

Why do you Mzungu [white persons] not try to understand the minds of Africans more than their ability to
work? You people do not understand; your words do
not belong to our minds.
MUKAHAMUBWAT, AN ELDERLY VILLAGE WOMAN
IN MAPANZA, ZAMBIA

S o would you like to invite Christ in your life, let him forgive your
sins and be Lord of your life?" was the way I usually concluded
my presentations of the gospel to the Hindus, Muslims and animists
in the city where I lived. Well trained in the formula of witness, I had
covered all the points. After five years of theological studies, during which
I'd gained a working knowledge of Greek and Hebrew, I could provide
answers to almost any objections to Christianity that came my way.

Yet by anybody's measure, I was a failure at introducing people to
my Savior. It was frustrating: I simply could not figure out why my
witness was having so little effect.

Looking back now, I suspect part of what was missing was an
understanding of shame and how it should influence strategies for
witness.

Individualizing the Gospel

When Westerners are trying to communicate the gospel to people who are sensitive to shame, they need to shift gears and express biblical truths differently from what they have been used to. Look back at the first sentence of this chapter's first paragraph. About every fifth word is *you* or *your*. In Western culture, where individualism is valued, the emphasis in evangelism is on *you*, the person, the individual—your sin, your guilt, your condemnation, your judgment, your decision, your eternity. Even as we quote Romans 3:23, "for all have sinned and fall short of the glory of God," we immediately personalize it with some statement like "That means you; you are part of the 'all.' " We do the same with John 3:16, "For God so loved the world": we ask the individual to fill in her or his name where the word *world* is. We do the same when we come to the word *whoever*.

This tactic is effective in an individual culture, where personalizing is important and understood. In group-oriented societies, though, focusing on an individual can be dangerous—especially if such focus exposes shame, failure or shortcoming. Thus rephrasing "all have sinned" to "you have sinned" may not be wise. Maybe where biblical writers used terms like *all, world* and *whoever* they meant to be indefinite or general in deference to a shame-oriented and group-oriented culture.

Shame, Sin and Culture

Missionaries and anthropologists tell us that many cultures have no clear concept of sin and forgiveness, especially where there is not a strong concept of God. In such places, however, there often exists a strong sense of shame (or "face" or honor) which can be built upon to share the gospel.

It might have begun with Adam and Eve, our distant parents, who were the first to struggle with shame in the Garden of Eden. The fall of humankind is recorded in Genesis 3, but the first mention of sin is in the following chapter, when Cain kills Abel. The imagery surrounding the

Fall is as relevant to the concept of shame as it is to the Western idea of sin. For example, before the Fall there was nakedness without shame (Gen 2:25), but after the fall nakedness brought shame (3:7) and prompted action to cover Eve and Adam's shame (sewing fig leaves into garments). The attempt to cover up shame (sin) is something with which we can all identify.[1] Some writers believe that this shame represents a primitive form of guilt, but perhaps that is simply a Western interpretation, since shame is also a New Testament concept (Rom 9:33; 10:11; 2 Cor 7:14; 9:4; Heb 2:11; 11:16; 12:2; 1 Pet 2:6).

The creation account reveals that shame has implications vertically (between the Creator and the creature) and horizontally (among the creatures, as with Cain and Abel). Much of this book has focused on the horizontal-relational implications of shame, but Scripture clearly casts the term in eternal perspective. Shame, in its ultimate sense, is the disruption of harmony between the Creator and the creatures, and the creatures' attempt to secure their destiny in a place other than the Creator.

Is this not the message of Paul to the Hebrew community at Rome?

What then shall we say? That the Gentiles, who did not pursue righteousness, have obtained it, a righteousness that is by faith; but Israel, who pursued a law of righteousness, has not attained it. Why not? Because they pursued it not by faith but as if it were by works. They stumbled over the "stumbling stone." As it is written:

"See, I lay in Zion a stone that causes men to stumble
    and a rock that makes them fall,
and the one who trusts in him will never be put to shame." (Rom 9:30-33)

The salvation-shame theme continues in the following chapter.

If you confess with your mouth, "Jesus is Lord," and believe in your heart that God raised him from the dead, you will be saved. For it is with your heart that you believe and are justified, and it is with your mouth that you confess and are saved. As the Scripture says, "Anyone who trusts in him will never be put to shame." (Rom 10:9-11)

What have we got so far in building our witness?

Like Adam and Eve, we are all exposed before an all-knowing and all-seeing God; nothing is hidden from him. He knows and sees our shame. The shame we experience results from our disobedience toward a loving and generous Father, who is also the Sovereign of the universe. Our shame is great. Our disobedience has broken the relationship with him and brought disorder into the world. We try to cover and hide our shame from him, but the fig leaves prove an unsatisfactory covering. Nothing we try will ever cover our shame. Our dilemma is most serious. We recognize the problem but are helpless to solve it.

The Father Acts to Restore Us

In a shame-based culture it is bad enough to be shamed before one's friends and colleagues, but to cause shame or be shamed before a father, elder or sovereign is exceedingly worse. Rupturing a relationship with one of great esteem and authority must be avoided at all costs. Normally the one causing the shame assumes the responsibility for restoration of the relationship. However, not only have we shamed ourselves and God but we are helpless to repair the damage, the future is hopeless—unless the other party chooses to act.

I quote extensively from T. Boyle, who explains the biblical application so well:

God has taken the responsibility for our shame. It is we humans that rebelled against God and broke the harmony of the family of creation. Thus, from an individualistic standpoint, it is we who should bear the blame and restore face before God but this is something that is beyond our power to do. Actually, God is in a dual position. As creator and superior, he must take responsibility for the condition of his creation. But as the "injured party," he must provide a way for mankind to "restore face." Throughout human history, mankind has been trying to do just that. Through a variety of ways man tries to cover his own shame before God. But, to use the biblical symbols, those efforts are all like "fig leaves" and "filthy rags." The broken harmony and shame it produced is so great that there is nothing we humans can do from our side to restore that original harmony. Thus, the initiative must come from God. . . .

How could God fulfill both aspects of his dual position as both superior and the one who has been offended? The answer lies in the mystery of the incarnation. To use the parent analogy again, when, as God's children, mankind broke the relationship he had with God through disobedience and "lack of filial piety," God, as parent, had to take responsibility for the condition of his creation brought about by his children's wrongful actions. A human parent in Japanese culture would go before the injured party apologizing with deep bows—even prostrating himself before the offended. This may even lead to a situation where a person of high social rank has to bow deeply before a person of low social rank and use the honorific terms of speech. Thus the cultural form for covering the shame is for the parent (or other superior in charge) to put himself in a very humble position.

How could the Creator God of the universe put himself in a humble position? It is a great mystery, but through the incarnation of Jesus Christ, God became a man and took on the form of humility.[3] Jesus Christ, "being in very nature God . . . made himself nothing, taking the very nature of a servant, being made in human likeness. And being found in appearance as a man, he humbled himself and became obedient to death, even death on a cross!" (Phil 2:6-8). This passage on the humility and servanthood of Christ follows Paul's plea for unity and solidarity among believers: "make my joy complete by . . . being one in spirit and purpose. Do nothing out of selfish ambition or vain conceit, but in humility consider others better than yourselves. Each of you should look not only to your own interests, but also to the interests of others" (Phil 2:2-4).

Jesus the Shame Bearer

The cross symbolizes the most shameful form of death. For Christ, the cross was only the culmination of a life of being shamed and rejected by the government leaders and religious authorities of his day. To bear shame for one's wrong is hard, but to bear shame for always doing right is an infinitely greater burden. But Jesus "for the joy set before him endured the cross, scorning its shame, and sat down at the right hand of the throne of God" (Heb 12:2).

The believers to whom Hebrews was addressed were debating whether they had made a mistake leaving the traditions of their families, friends and ancestors to embrace Jesus. Departing from one's group, one's heritage, brings scorn and shame—and it did so especially in the tightly knit, shame-sensitive, religiously confident culture of the Hebrews.

So it must have come as a particular encouragement to the doubting Hebrew Christians to have the writer of Hebrews rehearse the great people of their history (Heb 11). These heroes (Noah, Abraham, Joseph and the others), having embraced the faith, took their stand against group expectations and followed God's way, often to the contempt of others. Those who departed from the crowd to follow God were forerunners of Christ, who also "endured such opposition from sinful men" (Heb 12:3). So the writer calls his readers: "Let us fix our eyes on Jesus, the author and perfecter of our faith" (12:2), the one who knows what it is like to suffer shame. He is able to help "so that you will not grow weary and lose heart" (12:3).

The Christian church has a little-understood but very important obligation when a person from a shame culture becomes a Christian. It is not always wise or necessary for converts to break away from their family and cultural group; God may enable them to remain within the cultural patterns and established groups and work out their faith in that context. But if God calls a new convert out of a certain group and tradition in order to accomplish his purposes, the church must provide a strong community of support that will replace the relational networks the person has left behind.

If the church has an individualistic orientation, it tends to forget the needs of a new convert from a relational (also called "collectivistic" or "high-context") culture. Those from individualistic cultures simply do not realize the trauma of the terrible stigma attached to one who casts shame on family and friends by departing from the traditions. The new Christian accustomed to a closely knit extended family needs the church to become that new nurturing family.

Many of us are unaware of how much our culture influences us, and so the new convert may not realize how great an impact his or her conversion will have on relationships. Thus it is important that new Christians who have been reared in a group-oriented, shame-sensitive culture be told that they may experience severe rejection from family and friends. It is well to rehearse with this person that the ancestors of our faith (Heb 11) suffered similarly, as did our Elder Brother, Jesus Christ.

God has made us his children. Jesus calls us his brothers and sisters. Together we are family—the new family of God—and have confidence that "the one who trusts in him will never be put to shame."

Shame[4] is a subtle theme all throughout Hebrews. In 2:11, "Jesus is not ashamed to call [us] brothers." Before the Father, in front of all the heavenly angels and to every listening person, Jesus, so distanced from us in his deity, still proclaims his identity and solidarity with us as his sisters and brothers.

In 6:4-6, admittedly one of the more difficult passages for the Western theologian, the idea of shame—public shame—is part of the focus. "Those who have once been enlightened, who have tasted the heavenly gift, who have shared in the Holy Spirit . . . if they fall away" it is impossible for them "to be brought back to repentance, because to their loss they are crucifying the Son of God all over again subjecting him to public disgrace." "Disgrace" is the same Greek word for "shame," but here it is extraordinarily powerful in the sense of deliberate, open shame. The writer appears to be saying that one of the consequences of people's rejection of the Christian faith is that they will be adding to public contempt of Christ and making public mockery of his death.

To reject Christ is to add to the public shame already heaped upon him by his adversaries. Is this what they want to do to one who is God's Son, "the radiance of God's glory" (1:3), the one superior to Moses and the angels, the one who offers entry into the superior rest of God, the one whose person and priesthood are eternal, the one who brings a superior covenant, a superior hope and a superior sacrifice? It would be the worst travesty to subject Christ to further shame.

> Let us fix our eyes on Jesus, the author and perfecter of our faith, who for the joy set before him endured the cross, scorning its shame, and sat down at the right hand of the throne of God. Consider him who endured such opposition from sinful men, so that you will not grow weary and lose heart. . . . Make every effort to live in peace with all men and to be holy. (Heb 12:2-3, 14)

Summary

Harmony in relationships is an important social value. The violator of harmony bears the penalty of shame, disgrace and symbolic disfigurement. Rending the delicate social fabric causes one to become ugly before others. The only thing more frightening and repulsive to the shame-sensitive person is the prospect of having misplaced hope for the future. Erring in the securing of one's destiny is the ultimate shame, humiliation and folly. But the gospel offers a hope that will not disappoint.

> No one whose hope is in you
>   will ever be put to shame,
> but they will be put to shame
>   who are treacherous without excuse.
> Show me your ways, O LORD,

teach me your paths;
guide me in your truth and teach me,
for you are God my Savior,
and my hope is in you all day long. (Ps 25:3-5)

10

POWER AND WINNING: THE TWIN DISEASES

Successful communication with self and others implies
correction by others as well as self-correction.
JÜRGEN RUESCH

Winning qualifies as one of the more enjoyable experiences of life. Many of us win so rarely that we savor it for weeks when finally a success comes our way. Winning affirms some deep need within us all to feel significant, superior, right, exceptional, the best. Athletes express the exhilaration of winning as they leap high, wave their arms in the air and even weep. Such are the powerful emotions generated by winning.

It seems we all have some need to win. No one wants to be known as a loser. To always be second, never excelling, creates the feeling of being inferior, mediocre, second-rate—a loser.

Some of us, however, are *driven* to win. The need to win—the compulsive desire to be better than the next person and to make sure that one's superior strength, wisdom, beauty, knowledge or talents are evident to others—dominates such people. This need to win causes serious problems when it is carried over into relationships.

Few of us will ever enjoy world-class superiority in anything; it is the rare person whose name is a household word. We will probably never see our names lit up on a marquee. Nonetheless, we all have a need to feel significant, to excel in something, to be right some of the time and to be seen as making a meaningful contribution to the people around us. We feel diminished if authority figures, those we look to for help and guidance, always set themselves up as right, having superior judgment, knowing better than we do. In their presence we come to feel as if we have no worthy insights, no correct opinions and no ability to make wise choices.

Usually we respond in one of two ways. Perhaps we actually conclude that we are average at best, or worthless at worst; our self-esteem is damaged, and we resign ourselves to tedious mediocrity and low expectations for ourselves. Or we become angry at the way our self-esteem is being challenged and questioned. The anger may turn into resentment or even open rebellion. We may rebel by adopting values and activities exactly opposite to those of the "always right" authority figure. This response can be seen most frequently in relationships between parents and children.

In fact, this dynamic in the parent-child relationship can help us understand a whole range of relationships in which power, control and winning create tensions: for example, between Westerners (including missionaries) and citizens of other countries; ethnic conflicts in Eastern Europe; African-American and Anglo-American church and community relationships; and other relationships in the office, home, church, gang or factory.

A Story of Two Parents and Two Children

Darrel, a blue-collar worker, a Christian and a father, was blunt and outspoken. Some called him opinionated; others said, more gently, that he had strong convictions. Darrel placed a high value on being right and on associating with others who believed as he did. He also valued helping others to think rightly—that is, to think as he did.

Darrel had some winsome qualities: a sense of humor, an infectious laugh and a gentle smile that communicated peace to those around him. But if someone or something disagreed with him, he would quickly take a correcting posture.

Darrel's wife, Irene, was quieter and always supportive of her husband. Some looked to her as the model submissive wife. Darrel believed that wives were to stand behind their husbands' decisions. While Irene could express her thoughts, Darrel was head of the family, and his wisdom would prevail. In his view, this pattern fulfilled Scripture. To try to question or debate any of Darrel's decisions was to manifest insubordination, rebellion against his authority and therefore lack of submission to God's Word.

Darrel and Irene had two lovely daughters, Leah and Elizabeth—model Christians from all outward appearances. Over the years they rarely missed a church service. Their neat, scrubbed-clean appearance matched their Sunday-school lessons, which they always completed meticulously. Memory verses were recited word-perfect year after year. In class the right answers seemed to come naturally for them. Any parent would have been proud of their good manners, intelligence and charm.

Occasionally Leah, the older girl, would show signs of what her parents called an "independent streak," but her father would quickly challenge her behavior and show that it was unhealthy if not unspiritual. Once he had imposed his will, Darrel assumed Leah had learned her lesson. He and Irene were a bit concerned about the periodic outbreaks of independence, but they believed that God would prevail in Leah's life.

The girls were hedged about with rather strict rules as to when they could start dating, whom they could date, how late they could stay out and where they could go. In fact, most of their life was legislated; little was negotiable. They could not date, even in a group, until two years after their Christian friends did; they had to be in by 9:00 P.M. on school nights and 10:00 P.M. on weekends. No weekend dates were allowed until their Sunday-school lessons were done and their Bible verses perfectly memorized. If in any given week they were too busy to go to midweek Bible study and prayer, they could not go out that weekend.

Darrel was always right; the girls were always wrong. Sometimes he was right with sternness; sometimes he was right with tenderness. But he was always right, and any discussion about his decisions was short-lived.

Leah and Elizabeth's appeals to their mother when Darrel was not around brought the same results, but with more gentleness and understanding. "Father is the head of the house. He knows best. God has given him the authority. We are to submit."

Darrel earnestly believed that strictness, heavy control and making sure his daughters believed and acted correctly represented the highest form of love and eventually would produce wholesome, mature Christian women. He had good motives for his methods, and his aspirations for his daughters were noble. Unfortunately, good intentions, while necessary, do not guarantee good decisions.

As Leah, the daughter with the occasional "independent streak," approached graduation from high school, Darrel and Irene rejoiced. While they had gone through some rough spots with her, her parents were confident that all would work out well. They had little clue about the caldron of rebellion that was boiling within her.

After the graduation ceremony, Irene and Darrel returned home with Elizabeth; Leah had promised to be home "soon." But late that night, she had still not arrived; her parents were worried and angry. When they checked her room to see if somehow she had come home undetected, they quickly realized that she'd had no intention of returning home. Her clothes and favorite items were gone.

Totally confused, Darrel and Irene tried to figure out what to do next.

They tried to locate Leah, but without success.

Rationalization often sets in during stressful circumstances. "Satan had used her independent streak to get a hold on her," they reasoned. "That explains everything." They reflected on their parenting style but decided that if anything, they should have been stricter and trusted Leah less. Any error had been on the side of leniency.

Several months later, they got enough information to contact their daughter and find out what was happening. In essence, she had chosen a life of blatant sin and debauchery—the exact opposite of what her parents had hoped, worked and prayed for. Besides being confusing, this was a crushing defeat for Darrel and Irene. What had they done to deserve such a tragedy?

Before long, Elizabeth, their younger daughter, was also ready for graduation. She had been a model child, never giving her parents a minute's trouble. She was quiet, gentle, friendly, poised and confident; no "independent streak" had ever surfaced. Her parents had high hopes for her and let it be known that if she were to become a pastor's wife or missionary, that would make them very happy.

After her graduation ceremony, Darrel and Irene looked for her—they were ready to celebrate and take pictures. She was nowhere to be found. They became anxious. This was unlike her; she had always been so very responsible. Eventually they checked back at the house—and to their horror, they learned that Elizabeth, like her sister, had packed her bags and disappeared.

Darrel and Irene were heartsick. Their model child had been living a double life—one at home and church and the other at school. When their first communication from Elizabeth came nearly two years later, they discovered that she too had rebelled completely against her parents' ways. More confused than ever, they concluded that Satan was the great deceiver.

They had done their best—but all they had to show for it was heartache.[1]

POWER AND WINNING: THE TWIN DISEASES

Understanding Response Styles

Darrel and Irene had good intentions, honestly loved their daughters, desired the best for them, prayed daily and intensely for them, performed thousands of little loving deeds, and did the best they knew how. How could everything have turned out so wrong?

Part of the answer, I believe, will come to light as we explore an important part of communication—what has been called "response styles." Carl Rogers, a renowned psychologist, investigated response styles in person-to-person communication. He found that people's responses to others fell into five different categories, which I list here from most frequent to least frequent:

- □ evaluative
- □ interpretative
- □ supportive
- □ probing
- □ understanding[2]

Evaluative responses include some form of evaluation or judgment— some indication of right or wrong, good or bad, moral or immoral, wise or stupid, approval or disapproval, acceptance or rejection. Tone of voice and body language can communicate evaluation even if the words do not. An example of an evaluative response is "That music doesn't sound very Christian."

The *interpretative* response aims to ascertain the correct meaning of the other person's statement or behavior. It requests further explanation so that intentions and motives can be clarified. It is a way of showing the other person what effect their behavior or words have on you or others without appearing evaluative. For example: "I have been listening to your music; can you tell me the words and the message it is communicating?"

If the speaker's voice or body language is negative, the other person will sense evaluation, not honest interpretation. But a genuine interpretative response can be a good nonjudgmental way of confronting a person. It is less likely to bring a defensive response and more likely to keep communication lines open.

The *supportive* response is important when you want to communicate acceptance and let others know that you are favorable toward them. Encouraging, affirming, caring kinds of comments can help a person who is dealing with tough problems or stress and needs strength to move ahead. "You seem to really enjoy that music" is a supportive response.

Probing responses attempt to explore an issue through questions and leading statements. They are important when you need an accurate assessment, a clear understanding of the facts. Probing allows you to find out what you need to know before you can offer sound advice. Here are some probing responses that should not be threatening:

☐ What were your feelings as you were listening to the music?

☐ What thoughts or reasons prompted you to buy that cassette?[3]

☐ Tell me more about the music you are listening to. It seems important to you.

And a few probing responses on other topics:

☐ Tell me about your weekend [trip, summer, date].

☐ What is the best thing that has happened to you recently?

☐ What is the worst thing that has happened to you recently?

☐ Are you feeling challenged in your work?

☐ What would you change about your life if you could wave a magic wand?

☐ Why did you use that particular word—does it carry a special meaning?

☐ Why do you think this has affected you this way?

☐ When the other person did [said] that, what went through your mind [how did that make you feel]?

When someone is talking about a conflict, it helps to get him or her to think about what the other person is thinking and feeling. The following questions aim to help the person get the perspective of the other:

☐ How do you think the other person felt when you said [did] that?

□ Can you think of any good reason the other person did [said] that?

□ If you were in the other person's shoes, what would you have done differently and why?

I have given extra attention to this type of response because many of us try to do honest probing but come across as being evaluative. This causes our hearers to erect defensive walls, and immediately what began as an innocent inquiry turns sour. Later in this chapter we will see why this tends to happen and how we can keep it from happening.

Understanding responses, though least used according to Rogers's research, may be the most powerful response for building and sustaining relationships. Understanding requires good listening skills and communicates acceptance and safety to the other person. In this atmosphere thoughts and feelings can be freely shared. An important outcome of understanding is that each is able to achieve the perspective of the other, to see the situation as he or she sees it. The better we understand the other person's perspective, the more relevant will be our comfort, encouragement and advice.

One kind of understanding response is to repeat what you think you have heard. For example, "Let me tell you what I think I heard you say and tell me if I am hearing you accurately." Following are other responses that signal a desire to understand:

□ You must have felt very sad [happy, surprised, disappointed, frustrated].

□ Then what happened?

□ So you think that . . .

□ It seems to me that . . .

As you read this, you might think there are very fine lines between some of these response styles. That is true, but the important point is to realize that if we overuse one style, we will run into problems.

Forty Percent Equals One Hundred Percent

The five response styles are neither good nor bad. The two critical factors are how frequently a given style is used and the appropriateness of the style for the occasion. Both are important considerations, but Rogers made an amazing and profound discovery about the frequency of response styles. He found that if a person uses one type of response 40 percent of the time or more, people will think that she or he is responding that way 100 percent of the time.[4]

Consider the evaluative response, the one that is used most frequently. If a person uses evaluative responses at least 40 percent, others will perceive that person is making evaluative remarks all the time, even when he or she is *not* responding that way. When the person gives a probing or understanding response, others will still feel as though they are being judged or evaluated.

In the same way, if a father uses understanding responses 40 percent of the time or more, even when he gives an evaluative response (for example, "I think that would be an unwise decision; so do not do it") the child does not hear it as a prohibitive statement but as somewhat accepting. The child then rather freely violates the prohibition. The father, rightfully upset, may punish the child. The child is upset because she had not "heard" her father's strong negative (evaluative) response. But if the father decides not to punish or otherwise hold the child responsible for her disobedience, the child will have further cause not to hear his next evaluative response.

If this can be transferred into the context of winning, it follows that if I take a win-lose approach (see "The Win-Lose Strategy" in chapter three) 40 percent of the time or more, people will perceive me as *always* trying to win, to be right, to be superior, to be ahead. Unless we are able to exercise variety and balance in our responses, people will perceive us only in one mode.

And since most of us choose our responses at the unconscious level—that is, we do not stop to discern whether a situation calls for a probing, interpretative or understanding response—we may use largely evaluative responses even when the emotions underlying the response vary. Regardless of whether my underlying feelings are anxiety and anger or care and concern, evaluative words are still evaluative words. And the results will be similar—the other person will feel like the loser. For sure, losing in an atmosphere of sensitivity is preferable—for a time. But being (or seeming to be) continually on the losing end eventually generates resentment, anger and perhaps rebellion.

The Missionary's Power
The missionary, often without realizing it, has an enormous amount of power. *Education and knowledge* are power. Most Western missionaries have at least a bachelor's degree, and many are pursuing doctoral work. The one who knows more than others is perceived as having an inside track on what is right in the multitudes of daily decisions. *Money* wields a more subtle but still pervasive influence. The missionary is able to raise money, and those funds are channeled to people and projects that find favor in the missionary's eyes. The host-country person who disagrees too often or too strongly (that is, tries to win on occasion) may find the missionary's financial support evaporating. State-of-the-art *equipment* (vehicles, computers, fax machines, telephones, electronics) help consolidate power around the missionary. The person who controls the resources possesses the power.

Most missionaries, I believe, do not *consciously* try to control through these forms of power, but we easily slip into a controlling mode unless we consciously understand, manage and share the power that comes with our cultural baggage. Despite all our talk about empowerment of others, most of us (whether Westerners or Two-Thirds World peoples) find it very difficult to give up power. Power is a great seducer; it leads us into illusions about our centrality to the work of God. It also shelters us from facing our insecurities. As long as we use power to maintain a position of strength, we tend not to face our weaknesses and seek help, nurture and healing from brothers and sisters in Christ.

Power that comes from God first of all connects me to others in the body of Christ. In this body all the members need each other. So any exercise of power that separates me from deep fellowship with the community of faith is an aberration and is certainly not of God. If one member of the body tries to assert superiority and independence (strives to win), that member is deceived, and the entire body suffers from the deception.

Though I have been speaking specifically to the missionary context, the problem is certainly not limited to missionaries. It is a human problem. Each of us needs to be responsible within our own situation and to search our own heart.

Most of the missionaries and Christian workers I know are generous people. They share their knowledge, money and equipment quite openly and often sacrificially. My experience suggests that missionaries and other cross-cultural workers, once aware of the subtle seductions of power, become anxious to change, since their deepest desire is to faithfully serve Jesus Christ.

Generosity and Its Complications

Although generosity is a virtue, it does carry complications—especially in a cross-cultural context. Simply put, giving is power. It is power to control valuable resources. It is power to select who is to receive and who will not receive. Therefore, it is power over people. This power can make giving a source of liberty and empowerment of another; or giving can further consolidate power in the giver, bringing inevitable isolation from other believers.

Giving is easier than receiving. Yet without reciprocity, a relationship will continue to be one of donor to receiver, superior to inferior, person of power to person with less power,. The generous giver who rarely receives will be popular for a time, with a wide range of eager friends, but will be an alien to the community; in time he or she may even become an enemy.

Western missionaries find it difficult to receive from people in the

Two-Thirds World: "What do they have to give me?" Of course, such a question assumes that reciprocity requires some equal exchange of material things or knowledge. Many people in the Two-Thirds World have neither the schooling nor the material wealth to balance the scales in that way. Yet it is a Western limitation to think of reciprocity in such restrictive, materialistic categories.

"We Do Not See Your Heart"

Actually, reciprocity can be effected in intangibles as well as tangibles. I have found that the Christians of Africa, Latin America, Asia and other parts of the world desire a more open, honest, even intimate relationship with their missionary colleagues. Such friendship does exist, but it needs to be practiced more broadly.

When my wife and I led workshops throughout Africa, comments we heard repeatedly were: "The missionaries do not show us what is in their hearts," or "We are never allowed to see the heart of the missionary." As we probed for meaning, we found these Africans were saying that they were not allowed into the pain, frustrations, anxieties, heartaches or even the joys of missionaries' personal lives. Often missionaries share their personal lives only in missionary prayer meetings, carefully concealing them from their host-country brothers and sisters. One furloughing missionary reported in a moment of extraordinary insight and honesty, "I only let them look at my life, as it were, through a keyhole. They saw only a small part of me, and only what I wanted them to see."

I suspect the missionaries' motives are good and sincere: We don't want the people to see our feet of clay, for to expose our frailties would be to betray ourselves as inadequate examples. We want them to see us as model Christians. So we hide our pain, disappointments and failures.

But as a result, relationships in the body of Christ are superficial; we do not carry one another's burdens. And we are no longer fully human, no longer genuine. We portray only the most exemplary part of our lives while masking our deficiencies, doubts, aches and defeats. No one is fooled. Our masks simply keep all of us from having authentic, unhypocritical relationships. Without reciprocity no friendship exists—only a lopsided donor-receiver connection in which contacts substitute for relationship and benevolent oppression disguises overt control. Giving outside of genuine friendship can be perceived as a form of control and usually results in a dependency that turns sour for everyone.[5]

A reciprocity of honest sharing in each other's lives goes far in balancing out cross-cultural giving and receiving. The receiving and giving of friendship is at the same time the relinquishing of power and the empowering of the other.

Reuel Howe expresses this theme in another way:

Every man is a potential adversary, even those whom we love. Only through dialogue are we saved from the enmity toward one another. Dialogue is to love what blood is to the body. When the flow of blood stops, the body does. When dialogue stops, love dies and resentment and hate are born. . . .

Monological love enjoys only self-centeredly the feelings of a relationship. The lover exploits the beloved for the sake of the emotional dividend to be had. In contrast, dialogical love is outgoing. The lover turns to the beloved not to enjoy her selfishly but to serve her, to know her, and through her to be.[6]

May God help us all to discern our selfish and exploitive forms of "love" and replace them with the love described by Paul in Philippians 2:3-4: "Do nothing out of selfish ambition or vain conceit, but in humility consider others better than yourselves. Each of you should look not only to your own interests, but also to the interests of others."

Ownership and Control

Another frequent but mistaken assumption that leads to cross-cultural conflict is the notion that ownership of resources automatically entitles a person or group to have sole power of managing those resources

Missionaries usually hold ownership of key resources, and in Western thinking that implies the singular right to control how those resources are used. While we preach that God owns all things and we are only his stewards, we tend to operate as though we were actually co-owners with God. If in fact God does own all things, then they fall not only under my stewardship but also under the stewardship of my brothers and sisters. The disposition of God's resources should be seen not as an individual responsibility but as a communal trust.

I realize that this perspective makes us Westerners quite uncomfortable, but we must guide ourselves by Scripture rather than Western individualism or pragmatics. It may take some time to work out real shared responsibility, but we need to set our direction with the awareness that our fellow pilgrims from the Two-Thirds World are priests and kings with us. Without their collegiality and friendship we are most handicapped in bringing glory to God.

I do not want to be misunderstood here. I have never seen a missionary who is intentionally malicious and flagrantly exercises control over host-country people. But it is within the nature of all of us, when we have power, to believe that our ways are right. Power inflames egocentrism—the belief that my way of seeing things is the right way. When I firmly belief that I am right and possess the power to exercise that rightness, the slide into the mode of "I know best" is effortless.

When I am in the "I know best" mode, whether I am conscious of it or not, others must necessarily experience being wrong—having less knowledge, less power, less insight, less authority and less control over their lives. If people are put in this position on an ongoing basis, as Darrel's daughters were, anger and resentment build and eventually erupt in rebellion; the aggrieved persons may usurp power in an explosive and painful manner. Accusations fly, demands multiply, confusion reigns.

"What happened?" cry the missionaries. "We gave them the Word of God, education, medicine, church buildings, salaries. vehicles. We invested our very lives in these people, and now they turn on us. How could they do this after all we have done for them?"

But how did the host nationals interpret the missionaries' efforts? Perhaps they would say: "You always knew what was best for us and did not need to develop the deep relationships, mutuality and interdependence that are needed for healthy interaction, partnering and empowering."

This scenario is being repeated around the world as missionaries and national believers struggle to understand each other's motives and behaviors. I suspect it will continue to occur until Westerners realize the multitude of ways they are perceived as winning and begin to change their patterns. We must realize that we are prone to use evaluative responses and to assess the right and wrong of every situation.

Darrel and his wife were profoundly committed to their daughters; they showed love to them in many ways; they desired the best for them; they even sacrificed considerably so Leah and Elizabeth would have the best opportunity for success and happiness. It seemed to Darrel and Irene that they had done everything for the benefit of their daughters, but it all came to ashes. This is exactly how missionaries feel when the indigenous people's resentment and rebellion surface. Believing they did the best they could but still having to endure the trauma of angry rejection, already frustrated parents or missionaries are torn by confusion. Few sensations are more debilitating.

I have often heard missionaries say, "They [the nationals] want us to make the decisions—they ask us what we think and what they should do." I myself have experienced this deferring to my opinion, and I confess that it is heady to have others seek my advice. But what does it mean? Does it mean they value my opinion over their own? That they see my way as best? Probably not! Usually it means they want to show respect. It is an expression of courtesy in a culture where guests must be made to feel welcomed, significant and honored.

Thus many Two-Thirds World people are more concerned with

dialogue and relationship than with getting the right answer. If I respond with my "right" answer, the indigenous people feel some obligation to follow through lest they cause me shame by ignoring my advice.

Rather than giving advice, Westerners overseas might do well to use probing and supportive responses—that is, take a discussion approach rather than a telling approach. In such a way, they would not only achieve understanding but also allow others to work out their own conclusions, which would undoubtedly be more culturally appropriate.

I must fault the Western schooling system—including Christian schools—where task often takes precedence over relationships, individualism over community, goals over people, right answers over openness, inquiry and learning, and where service is defined more in terms of efficiency, accomplishment and power than effectiveness, being and humility. There is a tendency to believe that the more schooling one has had, the more one is qualified to give superior answers, to be right most of the time, to know best—even in a culture of people whose language one hardly understands. This belief, when expressed in relationships, chokes mutual freedom and smothers trust.

Again, in Howe's words: "The monological thinker runs the danger of being prejudiced, intolerant, bigoted, and a persecutor of those who differ from him. The dialogical thinker, on the other hand, is willing to speak out of his convictions to the holders of their convictions with genuine interest in them and with a sense of the possibilities between them."[7]

The person who needs to win is monological and will fight for a cultural version of truth, forfeiting the quality of relationships in which God's transcultural truth can be discovered and affirmed. God did not exclude anyone when he promised, "The Spirit of truth . . . will guide you into all truth" (Jn 16:13).

Summary
Westerners tend to use evaluative statements when responding to others.

If I give evaluative responses at least 40 percent of the time, I will be perceived as making evaluative statements 100 percent of the time. When those who have power make evaluative statements, they come across as dominating, controlling and needing to win. And when one party consistently wins, the other party develops resentment, anger and rebellion and will express such reactions as soon as the other party can no longer hurt them. To prevent this spiral of power struggle and resentment, Westerners need to learn to resist evaluative responses while developing interpretative, probing, supportive and understanding types of responses.

11
COMMUNICATION PRINCIPLES FOR CONFLICT RESOLUTION:
A CASE STUDY FROM JOSHUA

None of you should think only
of his own affairs, but each should learn to see
things from other people's point of view.
PHILIPPIANS 2:4 (PHILLIPS)

Near the end of the book of Joshua is found one of the most powerful conflict dramas in all of Scripture. The conflict broke out under the most unlikely circumstances and erupted with the velocity and destruction of a tornado. Civil war, a time when a nation sheds its own blood, is probably the darkest moment in any country's history. Such an event loomed on the immediate horizon for the nation Israel. The principles from this moment in Israel's history transcend time and circumstances.

The Story's Backdrop
The Israelites had wandered in the wilderness as homeless aliens for forty years. Moses had delegated to Joshua the task of taking Israel into

the Promised Land, Canaan. Joshua had led them to some spectacular military victories, not the least of which was the falling of Jericho's walls before them. The land God had promised was now theirs.

Finally they were home. No more living out of suitcases. No more breaking camp in the morning and moving on.

So the LORD gave Israel all the land he had sworn to give their forefathers, and they took possession of it and settled there. The LORD gave them rest on every side, just as he had sworn to their forefathers. Not one of their enemies withstood them; the LORD handed all their enemies over to them. Not one of all the LORD's good promises to the house of Israel failed; every one was fulfilled. (Josh 21:43-45)

With confidence that God's promises never fail, the fighting men of Israel gathered for the last time to divide up the spoils before going off to their assigned land, to their families, to peace. Hope filled every heart; the gathering was marked by joy and laughter.

Joshua summoned the tribes of Reuben, Gad and the half-tribe of Manasseh to receive their share of the spoils first. They had the farthest to travel—to the other (east) side of the Jordan River. Then Joshua gave them his blessing, with a farewell encouragement and admonition: "Be very careful to keep the commandment and the law that Moses the servant of the LORD gave you: to love the LORD your God, to walk in all his ways, to obey his commands, to hold fast to him and to serve him with all your heart and all your soul" (22:5).

It must have been a bittersweet moment for these soldiers. They had fought together, lived together and experienced God's miracles together. Deep bonds of friendship and brotherhood must have been forged. Picture these men embracing each other, kissing on both cheeks, perhaps with tears and promises to visit and write.

As the two and one-half tribes gathered their "great wealth" (22:8), they must have thought, "It doesn't get any better than this. Blue skies, friends around me, my family waiting, a secure future for the children and no more wandering in the wilderness. It's time to go home. Life is good."

The Beginning of the Problem

As they approached Geliloth, near the western side of the Jordan River, the two and one-half tribes decided to do something quite unexpected: they "built an imposing altar there by the Jordan" (22:10). Building a memorial was not unusual. Such markers were scattered throughout the land as reminders of some attribute of God or some significant event whose lesson the Israelites wanted never to forget. So building this altar seemed a good idea.

But the men of Reuben, Gad and Manasseh erred on two counts: (1) they did not build the memorial on their own side of the river, on their own land, and (2) they built it in the shape of a large altar. In fact, it looked like the altar in the tabernacle, which was the focus of the people's worship. God's law had made it clear that God's people were to worship at no other altar except the one in the tabernacle. But an outsider might reasonably assume that the men of the two and one-half tribes intended to use this new altar for worship now or in the future.

Word got back to the nine and one-half tribes, generating so much alarm and anger that they began preparing a military attack against Reuben, Gad and Manasseh (22:11-12). Several factors probably contributed to this hasty decision to launch a civil war. Foremost was the history of God's severe punishment whenever Israel had left the worship of the one true God and went "whoring after the gods of the strangers" (Deut 31:16 KJV). A similar warning had been given to the Israelites shortly before they ended their time in the wilderness; in fact, it had been given seven times in their uneven history and was given ten times after this event. No evil was more serious than to forsake God for another god. And that grievous sin was often symbolized by the erecting of another altar or center of worship.

Second, the two and one-half tribes had run into conflict with Moses years before over how the land was to be divided (see Num 32).

Third, the Israelite army had disbanded and now had to regroup to deal with this problem. Imagine that after seven years away from your family, you are finally going home—but your trip is interrupted by what appears to be a foolish and blatant violation of God's Word. Anger would rise easily. Dashed expectations provoke more discouragement and anger than perhaps any other experience.

Fourth, the men of Israel were fresh from battle against the Canaanites; this must have made it easy for them to opt for a military solution. Such a resolution would be quick and final so they could get on with their lives.

Amazing, isn't it? Only a few days ago the future had seemed perfect. As the frustrated murmurings fed irritation and passion for a hasty military settlement, the decision for civil war seemed irrevocable and the outcome inevitable. In war the two and one-half tribes did not stand a chance.

An Alternative to War

Although the text does not say, one can imagine some cooler elderly types standing apart from the young hotheads, thinking, analyzing, trying to understand, asking why. Perhaps one of those who pondered spoke up, calling first for quiet and then unfolding his thoughts to the others. After seven years of war, they were all sickened at the thought of more. He might have said something like this: "Maybe we are assuming too much. Maybe we don't have all the facts. Maybe we ought to talk to them." Perhaps this heroic but unnamed person remembered the Deuteronomy text that exhorts those who wish to know the truth to investigate, inquire, search, probe and ask diligently (Deut 13:12-14).

However the plan for dialogue surfaced, it made sense, and Phinehas, son of Eleazar, who was son of Aaron the priest, was chosen to lead the delegation. This was an astute selection. In an earlier crisis Phinehas had been instrumental in turning away God's anger from the nation after grievous sin. God had withheld his judgment because Phinehas "was zealous for the honor of his God and made atonement for the Israelites" (Num 25:12). Here is an important principle: when facing a conflict with potentially catastrophic outcomes, seek the help of the best person, one zealous for the honor of God and one with a proven track record.

So Phinehas and ten representatives, one from each of the nine and one-half tribes, traveled to Gilead to meet with Reuben, Gad and Manasseh. Their encounter must have been tense for everyone.

We don't know if we have the elders' entire speech or an accurate summary. As you read their words, put yourself in the place of the two and one-half tribes. Assume that the men of Reuben, Gad and Manasseh had not *intended* to commit a sin and that they had some rational reason for their actions. With this orientation, try to hear the elders' words as the original listeners might have heard them. Monitor your reactions. What do you hear? What are some characteristics of their communication? How do you feel about it? What might your reaction have been if you had been present?

The whole assembly of the LORD says: "How could you break faith with the God of Israel like this? How could you turn away from the LORD and build yourselves an altar in rebellion against him now? Was not the sin of Peor enough for us? Up to this very day we have not cleansed ourselves from that sin, even though a plague fell on the community of the LORD! And are you now turning away from the LORD?

"If you rebel against the LORD today, tomorrow he will be angry with the whole community of Israel. If the land you possess is defiled, come over to the LORD's land, where the LORD's tabernacle stands, and share the land with us. But do not rebel against the LORD or against us by building an altar for yourselves, other than the altar of the LORD our God. When Achan son of Zerah acted unfaithfully regarding the devoted things, did not wrath come upon the whole community of Israel? He was not the only one who died for his sin." (22:16-20)

When I have asked people what they hear in this speech, they report hearing mostly negative things. We don't know what tone of voice the representatives used or what other nonverbal messages they might have communicated, but when their words are analyzed at face value, the number of negative characteristics heavily outweighs that of positive ones.

Every day we analyze the characteristics of people's communication to us, usually at an unconscious level. Invariably we experience a natural emotional response. We have certain feelings about what we are hearing and about the person who is speaking. Following is a list of the emotions people have reported feeling in response to the Israelite elders' speech:

☐ Hurt and rejected
☐ Angry; bitter
☐ Fearful; threatened
☐ Falsely accused and unjustly judged
☐ Misunderstood and ignored
☐ Inferior; insecure

When asked, "What reactions might you have had if you were among the two and one-half tribes?" people have responded:

☐ Tell them to mind their own business
☐ Become defensive
☐ Retaliate and verbally attack them
☐ Find fault with them; criticize; point out failures in their past
☐ Try to explain and reason with them
☐ Walk away in silence; withdraw
☐ Try to work out a compromise

We can easily identify with most of these responses. But had the two and one-half tribes responded in most of these ways, the consequences would have been disastrous. Their response was a pivotal point: would they move toward bloodshed and war or peace and renewed respect?

The Crucial Response

My guess is that an extraordinarily wise person spoke on behalf of the two and one-half tribes, someone who

☐ understood the dynamics;
☐ could size up the situation quickly;

❑ knew what was at stake in his response;

❑ realized that emotions cannot be trusted in tense, charged situations;

❑ possessed the maturity to resist getting even and instead to pursue the truth;

❑ would speak neither from fear nor arrogance but from humble and quiet confidence.

If you had been designated spokesperson for the two and one-half tribes, how would you have responded? Take a moment to put your thoughts together. What overarching message would you want to send? What kinds of words would you use to make sure your fellow Israelites heard that message? How do you think the nine and one-half tribes would respond to your communication?

Here is the communication of the two and one-half tribes.

The Mighty One, God, the LORD! The Mighty One, God, the LORD! He knows! And let Israel know! If this has been in rebellion or disobedience to the LORD, do not spare us this day. If we have built our own altar to turn away from the LORD and to offer burnt offerings and grain offerings, or to sacrifice fellowship offerings on it, may the LORD himself call us to account.

No! We did it for fear that some day your descendants might say to ours, "What do you have to do with the LORD, the God of Israel? The LORD has made the Jordan a boundary between us and you—you Reubenites and Gadites! You have no share in the LORD." So your descendants might cause ours to stop fearing the LORD.

That is why we said, "Let us get ready and build an altar—but not for burnt offerings or sacrifices." On the contrary, it is to be a witness between us and you and the generations that follow, that we will worship the LORD at his sanctuary with our burnt offerings, sacrifices and fellowship offerings. Then in the future your descendants will not be able to say to ours, "You have no share in the LORD."

And we said, "If they ever say this to us, or to our descendants, we will answer: Look at the replica of the LORD's altar, which our fathers built, not for burnt offerings and sacrifices, but as a witness between us and you."

Far be it from us to rebel against the LORD and turn away from him today by building an altar . . . other than the altar of the LORD our God that stands before his tabernacle. (22:22-29)

When we gain the perspective of the other party and hear their motivations, a new picture of the situation often unfolds (see the verse at the beginning of the chapter). Now that we have the point of view of the two and one-half tribes, let's use imagination to fill in the few remaining blank spaces.

As the two and one-half tribes traveled toward their home, they became overwhelmed with the faithfulness and goodness of God and the fact that indeed there was only one true God. But then they remembered how easy it is, when things are going well, to forget God and put other gods in his place. And they began to discuss how they could protect themselves and subsequent generations from slipping away from Yahweh.

They realized how quickly rationalization and deception can twist one's thinking. The best intentions become diluted by pragmatics and base desires; soon we find a substitute for worshipping the one true God. "If it happened to us before, it can happen again, and it can happen to our children and our grandchildren," they reasoned. "That would be the greatest of all tragedies. Can we do something that would help protect us and our children from failing in our devotion to God?"

Was this the line of thought they followed? We don't know, but it seems consistent with the text—and with my own experience. I have often contemplated what I could do to guard my children's relationship with the Lord. That desire stirs in the heart of every Christian parent and often forces us to our knees in prayer.

The Lord Is with Us!

As Phinehas and his colleagues heard the explanation, "they were pleased" and declared, "The Lord is with us" (22:30-31). The group of representatives then returned to their people and told the story. "They were glad to hear the report and praised God. And they talked no more about going to war against them to devastate the country where the Reubenites and the Gadites lived." The altar was allowed to stand, "and the Reubenites and the Gadites gave the altar this name: A Witness Between Us that the Lord is God" (22:33-34).

Conflict can result in reconciliation and stronger bonds. But more important, conflict can forge a unity that shows that the Lord is God. Every time Israelites passed by that huge pile of stones, the truth that the Lord is God would enter their minds and they would be renewed in their commitment to "the Mighty One, God, the Lord."

Such a happy resolution does not come easily, but it should be the goal in every conflict situation. In preserving their unity, the Israelites declared that God was not only strong to save but powerful enough to keep his followers together. Few things are more destructive to a cause than fractured, schismatic relationships. As we saw in chapter two, God's glory is revealed not only through the lives of individual believers but also, and perhaps even more, through the peaceful and joyous unity of the church, local and universal (Jn 17:20-23; Rom 15:5-13).

Communication Principles for Managing Conflict

From the communication of the two and one-half tribes we can extract principles that will help us to reach the same unity they did.

Principle 1: Declare allegiance to God.

Effect: Both parties can share a common ground.

The two and one-half tribes declared their allegiance to God exuberantly by referring to him as "the Mighty One" (*El,* the God of power), the triune God *(Elohim)* and the God who is present and with us (Yahweh).[1] In the midst of conflict, it is good to assure one another that our relationship with God is foremost in our minds. To do that up front may dispel some initial suspicions that the other party has departed from the faith. Christians whose mutual trust is strained will do well to establish this common ground.

Principle 2: Be ready to be proved wrong.

Effect: Emotions are defused and brought under control.

After establishing their commitment to God, the two and one-half tribes made a remarkable statement: "If this has been in rebellion or disobedience to the LORD, do not spare us this day" (22:22). In essence they were saying, "You may be right; if you are, we deserve punishment." I doubt the nine and one-half tribes were expecting this disarming response. Usually people are not open to the possibility that they are wrong. But in being so open, the two and one-half tribes accomplished one very important thing: they brought emotions under control.

Emotions have a way of blocking out reason, better judgment and open communication. Intense emotions affect two parts of the human anatomy that are essential for communicating: the ears and the mouth. As soon as emotions take over, our ears fail to listen to what the other party is saying. They become blocked—especially when we feel the other is making false and serious accusations. The other part of our being immediately affected is our speech. Have you noticed how your voice changes when you are under stress? It becomes forceful and moves up in pitch. Your speech takes a defensive tone, and shortness of breath often sets in.

When emotions intensify beyond a certain point in conflict, they have a negative impact on communication; if they are not brought under control, they will have a detrimental influence on the outcome.

Principle 3: Send "I" messages rather than "you" messages.

Effect: Defensiveness is disarmed, and open communication becomes much easier.

You or *yourselves* is used six times in the five verses of the elders' speech: "How could you break faith . . . How could you turn away . . . If you rebel . . ." Several more times *you* is implied. "You" messages generally raise the emotional pitch in the other person and create defensiveness, for they tend to project blame onto others for our thoughts, actions or feelings. Consequently, a closed form of communication takes place: people do not speak to each other but hurl verbal assaults in hopes the other will surrender. In conflict situations even good friends are never more than a breath away from becoming adversaries. "You" messages can bring that misfortune at lightning speed.

When we are blamed, the natural response is to become defensive, which is typically expressed in either aggressive or withdrawing behavior. Aggressive behavior includes striking back, going on the attack, perhaps pointing out the other's past failures and deficiencies. Withdrawing means one quietly moves away without trying to clarify or explain. Often the withdrawing person buries the hurt. But the buried pain does not simply lie dormant. It may be expressed in passive-aggressive ways; it may ferment beneath the surface and build until it eventually erupts; or it may be internalized and allowed to boil inside, with no steps taken to deal with it. None of these strategies are healthy; none lead to a constructive solution to conflict.

In contrast, the two and one-half tribes used the plural of *I (we* and *us)* some thirteen times, plus another six times when they used the plural possessive, *our.* "I" messages provide a way of owning one's thoughts, actions and feelings. Sending "I" (or "we" if you speaking for a group) messages in a calm, reasonable way will increase the possibility that you can work out a positive long-term solution in the best interests of both parties.

Principle 4: Explain your reasoning.

Effect: Motives and intentions are clarified.

When confronted with behavior we do not understand, we tend to assign a negative explanation for the action or a negative characteristic to the other person. We slide into a negative judgment about the person well before we have the facts. Then when we confront the other person, we bring a closed mind, a biased attitude and accusatory words. When the facts of the other person's intentions are not available, we are generally unwilling to suspend judgment and live in short-term uncertainty; instead we attribute motives and characteristics, and these are generally negative, especially if the trust bond between us is not strong.

In part, this explains what the nine and one-half tribes did to the two and one-half tribes. Fortunately, the two and one-half tribes showed neither aggressiveness (attacking and retaliating) nor passivity (withdrawing), but chose to explain forthrightly why they did what they did. Understanding the reasoning of the other person clarifies motives and intentions.

Most conflicts in the Christian community do not arise from malicious intent or any desire to suddenly plunge into sin—at least this has been my experience. People's motives and intentions are generally good, pure and honorable. In fact, I have yet to find a Christian in the early stages of conflict who is motivated by malice. Malice and ill will enter after there has been a series of miscommunications and misunderstandings. Then people may resort to malice to try to balance the scales of justice, at least from their perspective.

So it will help if we can govern our attitudes in the following ways:

☐ Think the best about the other persons from the very beginning, even if their history is not perfect.

☐ Assume there is a good and reasonable explanation for anything you do not presently understand.

☐ Wait patiently and nonjudgmentally until you have access to the person who can provide the facts from her or his perspective.

☐ Refuse to engage in any negative speculation.

☐ Use "I" messages to foster open, nondefensive communication (for example, "I don't understand; I need you to help me").

Principle 5: Speak to the issue, not to the person.

Effect: Genuine understanding of the situation can be reached.

The nine and one-half tribes spoke to their kinfolk, ascribing rebellion and sin to them. Failing to address the real issue, they missed the point and brought everyone to the brink of civil war. The issue was the meaning of the altar: why had it been built?

It is easy to attack people and assign motives, but that only draws us into sin, since God alone qualifies as judge of the heart. We are responsible for managing conflict by applying biblically tested principles. And Scripture never gives us license to judge others before they have a chance to completely explain what was in their heart. To assign motives is to usurp a prerogative God jealously guards for himself (see Mt 7:1-2; Rom 14:1, 13; 1 Cor 4:4-5).

In uncertainty, leave the judgment to God, for he alone knows the thoughts and intents of the heart. Only with knowledge of the heart's intent can there be righteous, impartial judgment. If we become privy to that knowledge, we can humbly approach a judgment in the matter, reminding ourselves that our understanding of our own selves is at best imperfect; our understanding of another is even more imperfect.

So speak to the issue. Listen for motives. Strive for understanding. Be very cautious in judging another, for God may choose to judge us by the criteria we apply to others (Mt 7:1-2). Yet we seem to be allotted some form of careful judgment, according to Jesus' words: "Stop judging by mere appearances, and make a right judgment" (Jn 7:24).

Principle 6: Pursue understanding before agreement.

Effect: It becomes easier to work out a long-term resolution.

I have already talked about the value of seeking understanding, but this principle must be stated apart from other aspects of communication. Too often parties will seek agreement before they fully comprehend the issue. Usually this happens when one party wants desperately to avoid conflict and feels most uncomfortable that the other person may be upset. But agreement without understanding is really not agreement at all. In time the problem will surface again, because it was not properly managed in the first place.

For some time I wondered why the two and one-half tribes took so long to explain their case. They were quite repetitive; in my judgment, they could have said it all in about half the time. But brevity and concern for time are not virtues when it comes to dealing with conflict. Saying it several ways allows the other party to grasp the content of what we are saying. It is presumptuous to believe that our first words will convey to the other party exactly what we intend.

There *are* times—few, I hope—when agreement cannot be reached. Even then, it is vital that both parties pursue understanding so that both have a grasp of the other's perspective on the matter. In this context of mutual sharing of minds and acquiring understanding, agreement may remain elusive, but it is much easier to take our leave while holding the other in esteem and respect. Achieving thorough understanding is the prerequisite but not the guarantee of agreement and long-term resolution. Understanding without agreement allows the two parties to continue respecting each other, because motives, intentions and facts, as best they can be known, are all out in the open.

Principle 7: Pursue a win-win resolution.

Effect: Reconciliation is achieved.

The two and one-half tribes were not interested in winning the argument and putting the others in their place, though we might identify with that temptation. Instead, they handled the conflict in such a way that both parties could come out of it with their dignity and honor intact. Important values were protected, and the relationship was strengthened.

When the Holy Spirit indwells both parties, we must believe that a win-win solution exists if we are willing to put the time and energy into finding it. I do not mean that an agreement will always be reached. I do mean that both parties will be able to preserve what is important to them and yet maintain a relationship of mutual respect. Honoring God requires an uncompromising commitment to pursue win-win solutions, so relationships are protected while significant values are not given up.

Principle 8: Make unity a major concern.

Effect: God's glory is revealed.

Sadly, unity does not seem to have the same priority in our families, friendships and churches that Scripture gives to it. We see the fracturing of relationships in divorces, in parents' abandoning of children, in the splitting of churches, siblings' fighting and never talking to each other, in people's church-hopping when something does not go their way. When we make instant relationships, we can also dispose of them instantly.

But if the solidarity of the body of Christ means anything, any divisiveness reflects negatively on the one God our Father and Jesus Christ as the one head of the church (Eph 4). After all, if God is love, how is it that so many conflicts between Christians end in alienation, even hatred? If he is a God of power, how is it that we cannot solve our problems peacefully and without schism? The church is to be like the triune God: different persons, but never a disruption in unity. As we saw in chapter two, disunity is a negative reflection on the character and power of God.

It needs to be said that building the altar was not a wise decision for the men of Reuben, Gad and Manasseh. The memorial's shape, size and symbolism were dangerous, given Israel's idolatrous inclinations. And while the two and one-half tribes seemed to strive for unity in this situation, they did not have a stellar history. The nine and one-half tribes had some basis for being suspicious. We all bring a history to a conflict situation and people may have a right to be suspicious. But it is an act of grace when they do not judge us based on suspicions.

Yet the two and one-half tribes resolved the conflict appropriately on this occasion, and we are the beneficiaries. The altar they built was aptly named: "A Witness Between Us that the LORD is God" (Josh 22:34). Unity among people, especially when it is forged in the fire of conflict, confirms to a watching world that God is alive, that he loves us and that he has given his Son that we might have life. In essence, God chooses to reveal his glory through the solidarity of his people (again, see Jn 17).

The two and one-half tribes had some sense of the priority of unity as a means of revealing God's glory. Having this priority, they were able to wisely handle a difficult situation—and the result was that everyone reaffirmed that Yahweh is God. May we be diligent to follow in their steps.

12
PRINCIPLES FOR MANAGING CONFLICT

A good man does not argue; he who argues is not a
good man. . . . The Way of the Sage is
to act but not to compete.
TAO TE CHING

The superior man acts before speaking
and speaks according to his action.
CONFUCIUS

Conflict may not be pleasant, but it does not have to be bad. Quite the contrary. It can be the means for strengthening relationships, building respect, winning new friends and establishing credibility. In fact, conflict can be a significant means by which God does his work of maturing grace in all of us.

First Things First
Before we engage in any serious contact with the people of another culture or racial group, we need to realize that they may hold different cultural values and use different rules to respond to conflict situations. What does this mean?

First, it means that the majority of the people in the world value relationships above most other values. So building relationships of trust takes top priority. Nothing of significance is likely to happen if there is little trust. Most Anglo Westerners try to build trust by showing themselves competent in completing tasks, whereas others tend to build trust by spending time, including work time, together.

Second, most people do not separate the person from the person's words or acts. To criticize a person's idea is to criticize or demean the person. So statements like "Don't take this personally, but . . ." are likely to cause hurt feelings and alienation for people outside of an Anglo Western culture. Westerners tend to dichotomize between the person and the words or acts; we rather freely evaluate another's words, ideas or actions, believing that our comments are not personal and should not strain the relationship. For most people in the world, however, attacking someone's words or acts constitutes an attack on the person and is perceived as crude if not vicious. Words, ideas, acts and the person are an inseparable one.

Third, when entering another cultural context, we need to begin by observing, asking nonjudgmental questions, learning and seeking understanding. Above all, we must try to keep from thinking of cultural differences as either good or bad ("I like that" or "I don't like that"). Rather, we can think of them as curious differences that must exist for a good reason. Then we can try to find that reason.

Fourth, when with people different from ourselves, we need to be particularly careful about making evaluative statements, blame statements, "who-is-responsible" statements or comments that single out one person or group as the cause of a problem. When among Westerners, one may need to be more assertive, since they believe that "you get what you go for." Westerners are not as skilled at reading between the lines and interpreting people who express themselves indirectly.

Fifth, when in an ambiguous or conflictual situation, Westerners are well advised to set aside direct, confrontational strategies in favor of indirect ones. Be gracious, courteous, calm and patient. On the other hand, the non-Westerner among Westerners needs to realize that indirect strategies may be interpreted as devious and even deceitful, while forthrightness will likely be well received.

Sixth, the person who is getting to know a new culture will do well to build at least one good friendship and allow that person to be a cultural interpreter and cultural bridge-builder. It is best to find someone who is well respected in the community, church, office or corporation. This is the person one goes to for help in understanding ambiguous situations or handling a conflict. Work hard on the relationship for its own sake, but also because it may well mean the difference between success and failure for you. Friendship obligates people to help one another.

Once a strong relationship of trust is established with such a person, you may go to such a person with a problem and say, "If a certain person had a good relationship with postal workers and then they changed their attitude, became cold and distant, and gave this person poor service, what is this person to think, and what is the person to do?" Your friend is now obligated to help you because you have, in essence, said that you are confused and in danger of doing a wrong thing—embarrassing yourself. In essence you have given your friend permission to instruct you, give advice, be direct or intervene on your behalf.

Ten General Rules for Dealing with Conflict
No matter what kind of conflict you may face, and whether you are using direct or indirect methods for resolving it, take the following steps:

1. Ask whether this is worthy of attention or should be let go.

2. Make your approach one of concern for the person and for preservation of the relationship.

3. Seek understanding through inquiry before forming judgments and making accusations (blaming).

4. Separate facts from rumor, partial information, feelings and interpretation.

5. Consider how much stress the relationship can bear; this will help

you tell how much time and sensitivity will be required.

6. Put yourself in the other person's place and try to appreciate his or her perspective on the matter.

7. Address behaviors rather than motivation.

8. When you detect tense emotions or defensiveness, back up and give assurances of friendship and your desire to understand.

9. Frequently acknowledge and summarize what the other person has said to assure accuracy of understanding for both parties.

10. Believe a win-win resolution is possible if both parties can remain calm, understand each other's interests and negotiate with integrity and fairness.

Principles for Cross-Cultural Conflict Resolution

When in a Two-Thirds World situation, consider the following:

1. The degree to which shame, face and honor are core cultural values will determine how important it is to choose an indirect method.

2. If the other person has had extensive exposure to Western culture, sensitive directness may be acceptable, understood and not offensive.

3. All forms of confrontation should occur in private, if possible, so as to minimize any loss of face.

4. Familiarize yourself with the stories, parables, fables, legends and heroes of a culture in order to appropriately interpret their use in conflict situations.

5. Understand the various indirect methods used in the Two-Thirds World and be alert to which ones are used and under what circumstances.

6. Build a close relationship with a host-country person who will be able to help you interpret confusing situations.

7. Ask God for help in understanding and applying unfamiliar conflict resolution strategies.

8. Scripture is the final judge of all cultural forms; prayer and discussion may be required before some cultural expressions are embraced.

Let us be humble in acknowledging that Westerners do not have exclusive insight on all that is right and wrong. God is not restricted to Western ways, and he has not exhausted his wisdom and grace on North America and Western Europe. The God who authored diversity loves it, embraces those who display it and honors those who celebrate it.

But humility does not imply naiveté. People of the Word need each other to exercise collective discernment in interpreting the Bible, which stands as the final authority and judge of all that distorts God's glory in any culture.

And we pray this in order that you may live a life worthy of the Lord and may please him in every way: bearing fruit in every good work, growing in the knowledge of God. (Col 1:10)

Notes

Chapter 2: Cultural Diversity Was God's Idea
[1]G. Coleman Luck, *First Corinthians* (Chicago: Moody Press, 1958), p. 35.

Chapter 3: Handling Conflict the American Way
[1]R. H. Kilmann and K. W. Thomas, "Developing a Forced-Choice Measure of Conflict-Handling Behavior: The 'Mode' Instrument," *Educational and Psychological Measurement* 37 (Summer 1977): 309-25.

[2]Roger Fisher and Robert Ury, *Getting to Yes* (New York: Penguin Books, 1983), offers excellent advice in how both parties can achieve a win-win resolution.

[3]One such advocate is David Augsburger, *Caring Enough to Confront* (Ventura, Calif.: Regal Books, 1973), though he modified his position in a more recent book.

Chapter 4: Conflict and Cultural Values
[1]Carl B. Becker, "Reasons for the Lack of Argumentation and Debate in the Far East," *International Journal of Intercultural Relations* 10, no. 1 (1986): 86.

[2]Marvin Mayers, *A Look at Filipino Lifestyles* (Dallas: SIL Publications, 1980), p. 77.

[3]George M. Foster, *Traditional Societies and Technological Change,* 2nd ed. (New York: Harper & Row, 1973), p. 178.

[4]C. H. Dodd, *Dynamics of Intercultural Communication,* 2nd ed. (Dubuque, Iowa: Wm. C. Brown, 1987), p. 76.

[5]Chinua Achebe, *Things Fall Apart* (Greenwich, Conn.: Fawcett, 1959).

[6]Mary R. Hollnsteiner, *The Dynamics of Power in a Philippine Municipality* (Diliman, Quezon City: University of the Philippines/Community Development Research Council, 1963), p. 190. Quotation taken from Foster, *Traditional Societies,* p. 116.

[7]Ibid.

[8]Don Richardson, *Peace Child* (Ventura, Calif.: Regal Books, 1974), would be profitable reading in this area.
[9]Bruce Olson, *Bruchko* (Carol Stream, Ill.: Creation House, 1978), p. 130.
[10]Ibid., pp. 131-32.
[11]Ibid., p. 134.

Chapter 5: Mediation and the Mediator

[1]This story was told to me by Pat Copple of World Relief Corporation, October 15, 1992.
[2]I am adopting Paul Hiebert's definition of *Two-Thirds World* as broadly encompassing Asia, Africa and Latin America. Some people use the term *Third World*, but that has negative connotations and I prefer the demographic definition of *Two-Thirds*. See Paul G. Hiebert, *Anthropological Insights for Missionaries* (Grand Rapids, Mich.: Baker Book House, 1985), p. 9.
[3]David Augsburger, *Pastoral Counseling Across Cultures* (Philadelphia: Westminster Press, 1986), p. 183.
[4]Paul Matsumoto, "The Missiological Implications of Shame in the Japanese World View," master's thesis, Fuller Theological Seminary, Pasadena, Calif., 1985, p. 96.
[5]Ibid., p. 97.
[6]Ibid., p. 96.
[7]Ibid., p. 78.
[8]L. Romanucci-Ross, *Conflict, Violence and Morality in a Mexican Village* (Palo Alto, Calif.: National Press Books, 1973), p. 37.
[9]Matsumoto, "Missiological Implications," p. 79.
[10]Ibid.
[11]Kenneth Wuest, *The Pastoral Epistles in the Greek New Testament* (Grand Rapids, Mich.: Eerdmans, 1952), p. 41.
[12]Ibid.
[13]William Hendriksen, *New Testament Commentary: Exposition of Paul's Epistle to the Romans* (Grand Rapids, Mich.: Baker Book House, 1980), 1:98.
[14]Ibid., p. 174.
[15]Ibid., p. 175.

Chapter 6: The One-Down Position and Vulnerability

[1]Ted Ward, *Living Overseas* (New York: Free Press, 1984), pp. 76-77.
[2]Ibid., p. 77.
[3]This story was told to me by Joani Strohm at a Cross-Cultural Orientation Workshop in Newhall, California, May 1988.
[4]This story came from Pat Copple, World Relief Corporation, October 15, 1992.
[5]A. Phillips, "The Book of Ruth: Deception and Shame," *Journal of Jewish*

Studies 37 (Spring 1986): 1-17. G. Kaufman and R. Lev, "Shame: A Perspective on Jewish Identity," *Journal of Psychology and Judaism* 11 (Spring 1987): 30-40.

Chapter 7: Storytelling and Proverbs
[1]This story comes from Dick and Judy Anderson, as told in their workshop in Ethiopia, October 1992, and in conference notes recorded by Dick Anderson, December 10, 1992.
[2]R. Finnegan, "Proverbs in Africa," in *The Wisdom of Many,* ed. Wolfgang Mieder and Alan Dundes (New York: Garland, 1981), p. 30.
[3]Ibid., p. 30.

Chapter 8: Inaction, Misdirection, Silence and Indefinite Persons
[1]This story was told by John A. Corby Jr. in a paper submitted for DMS 880C, Cross-Cultural Interpersonal Relationships, Trinity Evangelical Divinity School, July 1992.
[2]Based on a story by W. Rodney White in a paper written for DMS 880C, Trinity Evangelical Divinity School, July 1992.
[3]Richard W. Hartzell, *Harmony in Conflict* (Taipei, Taiwan, R.O.C.: Caves Books, 1988), 1:365-66.
[4]Ibid., p. 317.
[5]Ibid.
[6]Ibid., p. 325.
[7]Achebe, *Things Fall Apart,* p. 20.
[8]Foster, *Traditional Societies,* p. 211.

Chapter 9: Communicating the Gospel Across Cultures
[1]This shame is not to be confused with the false shame often felt by abused children or adults who have been psychologically manipulated.
[2]T. Boyle, "Communicating the Gospel in Terms of Shame," *Japan Christian Quarterly* 50 (Winter 1986): 44.
[3]Ibid., pp. 44-45.
[4]There are over one hundred references to shame in the Scripture, indicating the substantial role it played in the cultural environment of biblical times.

Chapter 10: Power and Winning
[1]This account, while based on real-life events, has been modified for purposes of anonymity.
[2]D. W. Johnson, *Reaching Out* (Englewood Cliffs, N.J.: Prentice-Hall, 1972), pp. 129-31.
[3]If people dwell in the area of feelings, probe their thoughts and reasons, but

if they are in touch with their feelings, then probe in the area of thinking and reasoning.

[4]Johnson, *Reaching Out*, p. 129.

[5]Further suggested reading: Tim Stafford, *The Friendship Gap: Reaching Out Across Cultures* (Downers Grove, Ill.: InterVarsity Press, 1984), and Bruce Olson, *Bruchko;* a contrast to Olson would be Don Richardson's *Lords of the Earth* (Ventura, Calif.: Regal Books, 1977). Henri Nouwen's *In the Name of Jesus: Reflections on Christian Leadership in the Future* (New York: Crossroad, 1989) provides further penetrating insights.

[6]Reuel Howe, *The Miracle of Dialogue* (Minneapolis: Seabury, 1963), pp. 3, 7.

[7]Ibid., pp. 9-10.

Chapter 11: Communication Principles for Conflict Resolution

[1]See Arthur W. Pink, *Gleanings in Joshua* (Chicago: Moody Press, 1964), p. 404.

Bibliography

Achebe, Chinua. *Things Fall Apart*. New York: Fawcett. 1959.

Augsburger, David. *Caring Enough to Confront*. Ventura, Calif.: Regal Books, 1973.

———. *Conflict Mediation Across Cultures*. Louisville, Ky.: Westminster/John Knox Press, 1992.

Becker, Carl B. "Reasons for the Lack of Argumentation and Debate in the Far East." *International Journal of Intercultural Relations* 10, no. 1 (1986): 75-92.

Boyle, T. "Communicating the Gospel in Terms of Shame." *Japan Christian Quarterly* 50 (Winter 1986): 41-46.

Dodd, Carley H. *Dynamics of Intercultural Communication*. 2nd ed. Dubuque, Iowa: Wm. C. Brown, 1987.

Donohue, William A. *Managing Interpersonal Conflict*. Newbury Park, Calif.: Sage, 1992.

Doob, L. W. *Communication in Africa*. New Haven, Conn.: Yale University Press, 1961.

Finnegan, R. "Proverbs in Africa." In *The Wisdom of Many*, ed. Wolfgang Mieder and Alan Dundes. New York: Garland, 1981.

Fisher, Roger, and William Ury. *Getting to Yes*. New York: Penguin Books, 1981.

Foster, G. M. *Traditional Societies and Technological Change*. 2nd ed. New York: Harper & Row, 1973.

———. *Tzintzuntzan: Mexican Peasants in a Changing World*. Rev. ed. New York: Elsevier, 1979.

Gudykunst, William B., and Stella Ting-Toomey. *Culture and Interpersonal Communication*. Newbury Park, Calif.: Sage, 1988.

———. *Bridging Differences*. Newbury Park, Calif.: Sage, 1991.

Gudykunst, William B., Lea B. Stewart and Stella Ting-Toomey, eds. *Communication, Culture and Organizational Processes*. International and Intercultural Communication Annual 9. Beverly Hills, Calif.: Sage, 1985.

Hartzell, Richard W. *Harmony in Conflict.* Taipei, Taiwan, R.O.C.: Caves Books, 1988.

Hendrikse, William. *New Testament Commentary: Exposition of Paul's Epistle to the Romans.* Vol. 1. Grand Rapids, Mich.: Baker Book House, 1980.

_____. *New Testament Commentary: Exposition of the Pastoral Epistles.* Grand Rapids, Mich.: Baker Book House, 1957.

Hesselgrave, David J. *Communicating Christ Cross-Culturally.* Grand Rapids, Mich.: Zondervan, 1978.

Hiebert, Paul G. *Anthropological Insights for Missionaries.* Grand Rapids, Mich.: Baker Book House, 1985.

Howe, Reuel L. *The Miracle of Dialogue.* Minneapolis: Seabury, 1963.

Johnson, David W. *Reaching Out.* Englewood Cliffs, N.J.: Prentice-Hall, 1972.

Kagan, Spencer, et al. "Conflict Resolution Style Among Mexican Children." *Journal of Cross-Cultural Psychology* 2 (June 1981): 222-32.

_____. "Culture and the Development of Conflict Resolution Style." *Journal of Cross-Cultural Psychology* 13 (March 1982): 43-58.

Kaufman, G., and R. Lev. "Shame: A Perspective on Jewish Identity." *Journal of Psychology and Judaism* 11 (Spring 1987): 30-40.

Keil, C. F., and F. Delitzsch. *Commentary on the Old Testament.* Vol. 2, *Joshua, Judges, Ruth, 1 and 2 Samuel.* Grand Rapids, Mich.: Eerdmans, 1978.

Kilmann, R. H., and K. W. Thomas. "Developing a Forced-Choice Measure of Conflict-Handling Behavior: The "Mode" Instrument." *Educational and Psychological Measurement* 37 (Summer 1977): 309-25.

Lebra, T. S. "The Social Mechanism of Guilt and Shame: The Japanese Case." *The Anthropological Quarterly* 44 (October 1971): 241-55.

Leung, S., and Pei-Guan Wu. "Dispute Processing: A Cross-Cultural Analysis." In *Applied Cross-Cultural Psychology,* ed. R. W. Brislin. Cross-Cultural Research and Methodology Series 14. Newbury Park, Calif.: Sage, 1990.

Link, H. G. "Shame." In *Dictionary of New Testament Theology,* ed. Colin Brown. Vol. 3. Grand Rapids, Mich.: Zondervan, 1971.

Luck, G. Coleman. *First Corinthians.* Chicago: Moody Press, 1958.

Matsumoto, Paul. "The Missiological Implications of Shame in the Japanese World View." Master's thesis, Fuller Theological Seminary, Pasadena, Calif., 1985.

Mayers, Marvin. *A Look at Filipino Lifestyles.* Dallas: SIL Publications, 1980.

Motyer, J. A. "Mediator." In *New Bible Dictionary,* ed. J. D. Douglas. Grand Rapids, Mich.: Eerdmans, 1962.

Phillips, A. "The Book of Ruth: Deception and Shame." *Journal of Jewish Studies* 37 (Spring 1986): 1-17.

Romanucci-Ross, L. *Conflict, Violence and Morality in a Mexican Village.* Palo Alto, Calif.: National Press Books, 1973.

Samovar, Larry A., and Richard E. Porter, eds. *Intercultural Communication: A Reader*. Belmont, Calif.: Wadsworth, 1973.

Smith, E. W. *The Christian Mission in Africa*. London: International Missionary Council, 1926.

Spradley, J. P., and D. W. McCurdy, eds. *Conformity and Conflict: Readings in Cultural Anthropology*. Boston: Little, Brown, 1984.

Stewart, Edward C., and Milton J. Bennett. *American Cultural Patterns: A Cross-Cultural Perspective*. Rev. ed. Yarmouth, Maine: Intercultural, 1991.

Ting-Toomey, Stella. "Conflict Styles in Black and White Subjective Cultures." In *Current Research in Interethnic Communication*, ed. Y. Kim. Beverly Hills, Calif.: Sage, 1986.

_____. "Toward a Theory of Conflict and Culture." In *Communication, Culture and Organizational Processes*, ed. William B. Gudykunst, Lea B. Stewart and Stella Ting-Toomey. International and Intercultural Communication Annual 9. Beverly Hills, Calif.: Sage, 1985.

Walton, R. E. *Interpersonal Peacemaking: Confrontations and Third Party Consultation*. Menlo Park, Calif.: Addison-Wesley, 1969.

Ward, Ted. *Living Overseas*. New York: Free Press, 1984.

Waters, Harry, Jr. "Race, Culture and Interpersonal Conflict." *International Journal of Intercultural Relations* 16 (1992): 437-54.

Wuest, Kenneth S. *The Pastoral Epistles in the Greek New Testament*. Grand Rapids, Mich.: Eerdmans, 1952.